From
The Bleachers
With Love

Advice to Parents
with
Kids in Sports

David Canning Epperson, Ph.D.
and George A. Selleck, Ph.D.

Principles of Positive Sports Parenting

Copyright ©1999 by David Canning Epperson, Ph.D., and
George A. Selleck, Ph. D.

Library of Congress Cataloging-in-Publication Data:
Epperson, David C., 1932—
Selleck, George A., 1934—
        From the Bleachers with Love.—1st ed.
            p.   cm.
        ISBN   0-9672854-0-2
        1. Parenting. 2. Self-Improvement. I. Title.
        1999

This book is available in quantity at special discounts for your
group or organization. For information, contact:

Alliance Publications
P.O. Box 1429
Sugar Land, TX 77478

Phone (281) 565-2234
Fax (281) 565-2224

Designed by Jody Boles.
Copyedited by Janice Hunt.

ACKNOWLEDGMENTS

We would like to acknowledge the following people for contributing to the preparation of this book: Jim Kestner for his enduring enthusiasm for this project and his editorial expertise; Wendy Fayles for her helpful suggestions; the Saddleback Valley Volleyball Club parents, athletes, coaches, and administrators and the leadership of the AYSO organization for helping us identify the critical sports parenting issues; and to the many mothers and fathers who have attended our sports parenting workshops over the past ten years at the Volleyball Festival for inspiring us to share our advice with the larger community of parents with kids in sports.

*We dedicate this book
to our grandchildren—
from the bleachers with love.*

FROM THE BLEACHERS WITH LOVE
Contents

PREFACE

INTRODUCTION

PART ONE: CHOOSE A PATH

PART TWO: STUDY YOUR MAP

PART THREE: POINT THE WAY

PART FOUR: TAKE CARE

PART FIVE: BRIDGE THE DISTANCE

PART SIX: TAKE THE LEAD

THE SOCCER PHENOMENON:

"A Wonder of the Age"

One of the most encouraging new community activities in America, in *or* out of sports, is the neighborhood soccer leagues that bring men and women, parents and children, immigrants and natives, together each weekend in what Michael Elliott in the *New York Times Book Review* referred to as "a way that is a wonder of the age." This phenomenon was not planned by our political or business leaders. It seems to have *just happened.* It was not part of a communitarian master plan with origins in the '60s counterculture, although anti-authoritarian, anti-elitist, humanistic values have been advanced through emerging youth sports programs. Whatever the roots of this neighborhood-based, family-oriented movement, the outcome has been good for children, families, neighborhoods, and communities. The soccer mom was the creation of neither government policy nor market economy. Instead, she seems simply to have grown from the needs of the people for connective experiences, experiences that government, business, and religious institutions have been unable to provide. Neighborhood-based youth sports have emerged as an important connector, and we need to maintain momentum so that we create stronger communities where children and their families prosper.

This wonder of our age has often contributed to making sports families into more equal partnerships. Since in America, neither mothers nor fathers enjoyed the benefits of participating in youth soccer when growing up, and professional and college soccer are not a part of our regular TV fare, the balance of power as it relates to soccer shifts from one dominated by dads to one shared by moms, dads, and children. Unlike Little League baseball or Pop Warner football—where fathers typically possess more experience—mothers of soccer players are just as likely to have played as fathers. In fact, the children themselves are often the true family soccer experts. And since moms so frequently transport their children to practice and competition, their soccer expertise often exceeds Dad's. This sharing of expertise truly makes sports a family affair. But genuine sports families should not exist only in soccer; they should be the goal for all youth sports, in schools, clubs, and at recreation centers across the nation.

We have assembled this Positive Sports Parenting package, which includes this book and a companion workbook, to provide you, the sports parent or program leader, with the foundation for an ongoing dialogue about how families can get the most out of sports experiences. Sports are so much more than keeping kids off the streets. Well-orchestrated youth sports programs have the potential of renewing the spirits of participants, teaching life's lessons, and strengthening family and community ties. While this "wonder of our age" may have *just happened*, you can capitalize upon it to provide a much needed prescription for healing many of the fractures that modern life has created. We developed this package with an eye toward helping you speed up the momentum of a potentially powerful social movement whose time has come at last.

INTRODUCTION
Creating Positive Sports Opportunities

You can take initiatives to ensure that your family takes full advantage of the opportunities sports offer to enrich their lives.

Over 35 million boys and girls participate in youth sports. That adds up to a tremendous potential—the potential of sports to provide your family with unique opportunities to enrich your lives together.

If your child participates in youth sports, you can use those experiences to

- promote important values;
- learn about yourself and help your children learn about themselves;
- influence your children's behavior;
- strengthen family ties; and
- build connections with others.

Many of the problems that young people and their families experience today can be addressed when you learn how to use sports to strengthen family life. To succeed, you need to develop skills that allow you to make the most of your family's sports experiences. You also need to take an active role in shaping sports policies and practices to better meet your family's needs.

What are the keys to effective sports parenting in today's changing world? Let us take a look at six keys to positive sports parenting.

SIX KEYS TO POSITIVE SPORTS PARENTING

(1) Choose a Path. Have talks with your children to decide how much each of you wishes to invest in sports. To get the most from sports, you and your children must make significant commitments of time, energy, and sometimes even money. Working with your children to identify family goals will help clarify what you each hope to gain from your sports experiences. During these talks, also consider how the coach's ambitions might affect the achievement of your family objectives.

Example: You have visions of college athletic scholarships dancing through your head, but after talking with your daughter, you learn that her main reason for playing volleyball is to have fun with her friends. She sees the work involved in becoming a scholarship-caliber athlete as something that would take the fun out of playing. You also learn that your daughter's coaches are focused primarily on winning, which sometimes conflicts with your daughter's goals of just having a good time with her friends.

(2) Study Your Map. Most parents carry mental "maps" that reflect their own good and bad sports experiences. These "maps" usually include hidden or unconscious places you have visited or want to revisit. Your children's involvement in sports gives you the chance to call up these "maps" and learn about yourself—how your unfulfilled dreams about sports are influencing your goals for your children and how these missed opportunities affect your relationships with them.

Example: After reflecting on your own experience as someone who loved baseball but was always the last one picked for the team, you realize you have been pushing your son to be good in baseball as a way of making up for your own lack of ability—not as a way of helping him fulfill his own interests and desires.

(3) Point the Way. Sports provide you with unique opportunities to guide your children as they face decisions about how to meet the challenges of athletic competition. Use these opportunities as a laboratory for teaching many of life's lessons—lessons about hard work, discipline, teamwork, setting goals, and more.

Example: Your daughter has been the first to arrive and last to leave since the first day of tennis practice. She has practiced on her own and has given up chances to hang out with her friends because she wants to contribute to the team. But when her coach posts the list of those who will represent the team at the first big match of the year, your daughter's name is on the list of backups. Use this kind of setback to teach her how to deal with emotions such as fear, anger, and disappointment.

(4) Take Care. Sports can provide your family with opportunities to share special moments that uplift your spirits and strengthen family bonds. On the other hand, some sports experiences can threaten the physical, psychological, and moral well-being of your children. You need to be both supportive and protective as you monitor your children's sports programs.

Example: Your son's football team has a long-standing rivalry with another team. Each year, the competition has become more mean-spirited. This year, you decide to do something about it. You talk to some parents from the other team and organize a pre-game picnic that features a three-legged race pairing athletes and parents from opposing sides. Afterwards, you notice that the game is still competitive, but more enjoyable for everyone.

(5) Bridge the Distance. Sports provide your family with opportunities to build bridges between individuals of different gender, race, ability, and geographic and economic situation. However, you should not just leave those connections to chance. Actively plan how your children can develop new ways to connect with those different from them.

> *Example:* Old gender role stereotypes have historically limited both men and women, but can be transformed in a sports context. Girls can learn to take pride in being strong and displaying competitiveness on the playing field. Boys can learn to become less focused on dominating an opponent and more focused on enjoying the process of playing sports. These changes do not just "happen," though. They have to be nudged along by you, other parents, and sports educators who are sensitive to the changing nature of social expectations for men and women.

(6) Take the Lead. Parents who get involved in youth sports are often asked to serve as team chaperones, team administrators, coaches, or referees. This commitment means more than springing for pizza when the team wins! It represents your golden opportunity to get a closer look at your child's sports program; help shape the team's values; and help your own children as well as others learn from sports.

> *Example:* One of your jobs as chaperone is to help drive kids to and from basketball games and practices. You

develop a set of ground rules to govern the conduct of players while they are in your car. These rules reflect the coach's values as well as your own family values, and include such things as, "Show respect; no making fun of anyone on your team or the other team," "Focus on improvements; no dwelling on mistakes," and "Focus on performance; no whining about losing." (Discuss these rules with the coach before implementing them.)

PART
1

Choose a Path

CHARTING YOUR FAMILY'S SPORTS FUTURE

*To build sports experiences that promote
athletic success and enhance family life,
you must collaborate with your children and
their coaches to set challenging, achievable goals.*

In this section we offer advice to help you align your children's sports experiences with your basic family values. We show you how to get your family started on the path to an enriching sports future by helping you clearly define the values that your family wishes to promote through your experiences in youth sports. In addition, we discuss how you can teach your children to understand themselves and become effective advocates for their own interests. Finally, we deal with some of the challenges and problems that could cause your children to stray from the path that they have chosen.

YOUR FAMILY SPORTS CULTURE

How does your family view sports? Casually, like an occasional neighborhood softball game? Or does your day planner tell a story of volleyball games and basketball practices?

Every family has its own sports culture, made up of the personal experiences of the various family members. Sometimes this culture stretches back for several generations. One family that comes to mind is the Kennedys. They are not just famous for the various presidents, senators, and other politicians they have fostered. They are also well known for the competitive family football games they hold at the Kennedy compound in Hyannis Port. Over the generations, these games have become an important part of their family culture, where family values are reinforced and family ties strengthened.

Understanding your family sports culture is important because it affects the decisions you will make about the role of sports in your family's life. To show you how this works, we will describe four different cultural types. We do not intend the types to portray real-life families. In fact, your family likely reflects a combination of the values and traditions described in these examples.

Sports the Battleground: Good Winners and Losers

Families who see athletes as noble warriors tend to justify their investment in sports as an opportunity for their children to learn how to face the challenges of competition and become respectful winners and gracious losers.

Positive: A family guided by the battleground model often encourages everyone to become their best. They frequently see sports as a way to earn a college scholarship.

Negative: Warrior families sometimes become obsessed with winning. Such a narrow focus may result in neglecting other opportunities for personal satisfaction and growth and failing to value the efforts of those who do not excel. Focusing too much on winning may damage family life and the family's relationships with others in the sports community.

Sports the Classroom: Good Learners

Families who see sports as learning experiences tend to justify their sports involvement by citing its potential to teach life lessons. Winning is important, but not as important as preparing athletes to succeed in life.

Positive: These families see the playing field as a place where children can learn to become effective leaders and followers; resolve conflicts; recover from setbacks; and discipline, motivate, and coach themselves.

Negative: Parents often assume their child will automatically learn life skills through playing sports. However, unless parents and coaches help athletes see how sports knowledge and skills apply to real-life situations, the athletes will probably fail to make the transfer.

Sports the Village: Good Friends and Citizens

Families who see athletes and teams as belonging to the community believe involving their children in sports will help them become better family members, friends, and citizens. They see the playing field and social activities surrounding it as good places to discover and build common values that can strengthen family, neighborhood, and community ties.

Positive: These families emphasize the importance of civility, respect, and looking after others.

Negative: Critics say this kind of family culture makes it harder for athletes to develop competitiveness. Athletes who move on to college and professional sports may have impaired abilities to adapt to sports as a "business."

Sports the Sanctuary: Joyful Ritual

Families guided by an image of sports participants as celebrants in joyful community rituals view sports as a way to uplift and renew their spirits. They see the playing field as a sanctuary—a place to get away from the ugly stresses and strains of everyday life. For them, the creation of beautiful, joyful, memorable sports moments takes center stage.

Positive: These families feel less concern over who wins or loses and more with the rituals of sports—annual tailgate parties, the ceremonial oiling of the glove each spring, the neighborhood Thanksgiving Day "snow bowls." These rites of encouragement, enrichment, and enchantment offer participants food for their souls.

Negative: Families who view sports as a sanctuary risk being viewed as out of touch with the realities of today's sports world.

Principles of Choosing a Path

1

DETERMINE YOUR FAMILY SPORTS VALUES

Determine the values you want to maintain and
develop through your children's sports participation.

Why is it important to know your family's sports
values? Like an inner compass, our values guide and direct us
in all that we do. When we make decisions or participate in
activities aligned with our values (when we follow our inner
compass), we feel a sense of peace or "rightness" in what we
do. However, a decision or activity that violates our values system—no matter how much we may think we want it—usually
leaves us feeling uneasy or disturbed.

Childhood is a time of many decisions. It is also the time when we form most of our values. Children who have a clear understanding of their values will have an easier time when it comes to making decisions later—and many of those decisions will have a major impact on their lives.

The competitive nature of sports often places children in situations where they need to make immediate, values-based decisions: No one's looking—should I cheat? My opponent is favoring his right leg—should I hit him hard there on the next tackle? This girl really beat me badly at tennis—do I have to shake her hand?

Even sports decisions that are not so immediate still frequently involve an athlete's value system. For example, after quarterback Steve Young signed his first professional contract (with the now-defunct USFL for $40 million), he cried on his flight back home because he was afraid all that money would affect a values system that he had spent a lifetime developing. Many years later, Young's exemplary performances on the field and extensive charity work off it have shown that he has held true to his values.

To help your children make the right decisions in sports (and life) situations, you need to clearly communicate your own values and help your children understand what they value themselves. As a whole, your family needs to determine which values you want to maintain and/or develop through sports. For example, consider making a list of values like the one that follows, then discuss which are most important. Your next step might include talking about how sports participation affects your values.

Sportsmanship	Honoring Commitments
Family First	Honesty
Being a Good Friend	Hard Work
Loyalty	Kindness
Supporting/Encouraging Family Members	

Values are too important to be left to chance. By making a conscious effort to discuss and determine family sports values, you can better ensure that your family's sports experience is a positive one for everyone involved.

2

INCLUDE SPORTS ISSUES IN FAMILY MEETINGS

A child's sports participation will likely affect
your entire family. Conduct family meetings that
give everyone a chance to share their views
and give you the opportunity to guide your
children through difficult times.

Your child's decision to participate in sports will affect
everyone in your family. Wise parents recognize the impact of
sports on everything from dinner plans to birthday parties and
make it a habit to hold regular family meetings, avoiding the
"Wait-a-minute-I-thought-YOU-were-supposed-to-pick-him-up!"
syndrome and providing a forum for discussing important
issues that arise before, during, and after the sport season.

Family meetings are important for more than just keeping your schedules straight. Subjects to discuss at family meetings might include

- How sports involvement affects school, family, and social commitments;
- How the family budgets time for sports participation;
- The pros and cons of joining a sports training program;
- The physical, social, and psychological payoff of the sports "investment";
- How much sports participation will cost and how that impacts the family's approach to a given sport; and sometimes
- Whether the child wishes to continue participating at all.

There are times when parents will choose to make sacrifices so that their children can pursue their sports dreams; there are also times when family priorities should take precedence over a child's preferences. Family meetings give parents and children the opportunity to maintain a healthy balance between accommodating and denying. These meetings help children understand the necessity of taking other people's needs into consideration, the importance of being a team player, and the fact that sometimes we have to make sacrifices for others.

To make family meetings effective, everyone must have the authority to participate in the decisions. However, it is up to you, the parent, to set boundaries for those decisions (and deal with the anger and rejection that are often heaped upon the boundary-setter). For example, you might say, "You can choose which sport you want to participate in; however, we do not have the money to pay for more than one sport during the school year."

As a parent, you also hold responsibility for enforcing the decisions that are made in family meetings. Be fair but firm. Open your mind to evaluate new "evidence" your child might submit, evidence to support a change of plan. Following with the previous example, your daughter might respond, "But Mom, I have saved up enough money to pay for everything I need. I don't know what sports I'm going to like the most and want to try more than one. If I use my own money to pay for the others, can I go out for more than one?" You may decide that under these circumstances, you will support her decision. But be sure to hold your daughter to the original agreement. If she comes back later and wants to use the money for something else, you may need to remind her that doing so means giving up a sport. If you fail to follow through with your original agreement, your credibility will be destroyed. Perhaps more importantly, you lose an opportunity to teach your child one of life's most important lessons: "Be true to your word."

3

INVOLVE MOMS AND DADS IN SPORTS DECISIONS

*The voices of both mothers and fathers need
to be heard in family sports decision-making.*

Most families tend to look to fathers for decisions about the role of sports in the lives of children, since fathers traditionally have more experience. However, the family benefits the most when both partners take an active role in making these decisions.

Because women traditionally come from a background where achieving harmony in their homes and families is important, they tend to focus more on the aesthetic and social aspects of sports. They want to know how the sports experience will impact their children's self-esteem and relationships with others. They also feel less comfortable with the "tough love" approach of many coaches.

Men typically focus more on the "scoreboard," or achievement, aspect of sports: Did you win or lose, and by how much? Men also feel more comfortable with the "command and control" approach to sports training, since many of them have experienced it themselves.

Your family should consider both perspectives when making decisions that affect your children's sports participation. It is essential that you support your children as they chase their sports dreams, but your children also need to be reminded from time to time not to forget their hearts when they pick up their headgear. Children need to learn the value of achievement, but they also need to learn that achievement should not come at the expense of personal and/or family values. To ensure your children learn these valuable lessons, both mother and father should be knowledgeable about the games your children play—including the rules of the games, the fine points of competition, and the values promoted within the sports culture.

4

LET YOUR CHILDREN'S SPORTS DREAMS BE THEIR OWN

Consider your children's views along with those of both parents in family sports decision-making sessions.

As every parent knows, conflicts with their children are inevitable. In fact, for a child to establish individuality, she or he needs to test the limits of child-parent relationships.

This "testing" period is an uncomfortable time for both parents and children. As a parent, you may find that your helpful suggestions meet with a decided lack of enthusiasm. Your children probably feel that you frequently ignore their preferences. This conflict may result in hurt feelings on both sides.

You may find it challenging to avoid stepping in to make decisions that you know will make your child's life easier. What you may overlook, though, is that learning to make good decisions is like most other parts of life: It gets better with practice.

For children to develop into independent adults, it is essential that you provide them with practice in making decisions, and deciding how to use their time in sports, as well as in other areas of their lives, is an excellent opportunity to do just that.

For example, you should let your son decide how deeply he wants to get involved in sports. You may feel that he needs to spend more time practicing, take his membership on the team more seriously, or commit more to working hard on the playing field, but none of these things will happen until your son feels the same way.

If your children need to be badgered to make a greater commitment to a sport, then that sport may not be the most appropriate activity for them to pursue, even if they have the ability to be successful. If you want your children to succeed in their life pursuits, they must choose their own paths. Success in and out of sports takes great commitment, and the tenacity to achieve it only comes with something your children have chosen themselves.

We do not mean that you should avoid trying to pass a passion for sports on to your children. Just remember that *modeling* a strong commitment to sports is nearly always more effective than trying to *push* your children into something they show little interest in. In other words, lead your children by showing how much fun sports are for you, giving them opportunities for a variety of sports experiences, and encouraging all of their efforts.

You and your children should reach understandings about the role of sports in their lives before the season begins. When differences of opinion do arise, both you and your children have every right to express your opinions and preferences. One of the best times to do so is during family meetings, where all of you are less likely to feel defensive. If an issue cannot wait until the next regularly scheduled meeting, then arrange for a special meeting in a quiet place without distractions, helping everyone focus their full attention on the discussion.

5

UNDERSTAND THE COMMITMENT
REQUIRED BY THE COACH

Parents, coaches, and athletes should reach
understandings about training and competition
schedules BEFORE a sport season begins.

Parents, coaches, and athletes should reach understandings about training and competition schedules *before* a
sport season begins.

When coaches are asked to name the biggest headaches
of their jobs, "unreasonable and demanding parents" usually
soars high on the list. By the same token, parents frequently
put "unreasonable and demanding coaches" at the top of their
list of dissatisfactions with their family's sports experiences.

Many of the problems that coaches and parents experience with each other could be avoided with clear communication before the sport season begins. Ideally, the coach would

not only take the time to explain the goals, objectives, and expectations of his or her program to athletes and parents, but would also seek input in some of the decisions that affect athletic policies and practices.

However, like most of us, coaches are busy people. More and more coaches are walk-ons, which means they have other full-time jobs and just come after school to perform their coaching duties. Between the coach's schedule and the busy schedules of athletes and parents, finding time to coordinate efforts is difficult at best.

In addition, few coaches have any training in how to conduct a program that reflects the views of athletes and parents. Suffering from too many painful experiences with parents who are out to promote their own children at any cost—to the coach or anyone else connected with the team—coaches are also generally wary of having athletes or parents too involved in making decisions about issues that affect their programs.

We are not suggesting that you and your children should make coaching decisions. However, you do need to take your share of responsibility for achieving a clear understanding about training and competition schedules, expectations, program policies, and so on, before the season begins. If your child's coach fails to get information out, consider volunteering to help, for example, by writing and/or distributing letters or newsletters or scheduling and promoting parent/coach meetings.

Because excluding athletes and parents from determining sports policies and practices does a disservice to everyone, you need to assert yourself to make sure that your children's and family's concerns are heard. You and your children are stakeholders just as important to the institution of sport as coaches; therefore, you deserve a voice.

6

HELP YOUR CHILDREN BECOME
ADVOCATES FOR THEIR INTERESTS

Help your children develop the skills they need to work
effectively with decision-makers and authority figures.

Good coaches, like all good leaders, have a passion
for what they do, and they want their athletes to share that
passion. That desire often leads coaches to do things to encourage student-athletes to focus exclusively on their sport—
and sometimes leads coaches to feel threatened by athletes
who want to participate in activities that might take away from
it.

For some student-athletes, focusing on one sport is not a
problem. However, others have the ability and desire to successfully participate in a variety of activities at the same time.

What should you do when conflicts are created by competing demands on your children's time and loyalty? What skills do your children need to resolve the conflict in a way that will not compromise their positions with the coach or the director of another highly desirable activity?

When your children face decisions about where to invest their time, it is important that you equip them with skills that allow them to negotiate workable solutions that keep their options open. Think of them as "managing up" skills.

To help your children learn how to "manage up," you first need to teach them how to understand the points of view of the coach and others who are placing demands on them. To effectively negotiate with their coach, your children need to communicate that they genuinely understand the coach's position. Once they have done so, they can work to help the coach understand their position. You can help your children practice "managing up" by role-playing. A good start is for you to play the "child" and your child to play the "coach." Try out different scenarios of how the conversation might go to increase your children's confidence. This approach helps your children (1) to gain a better understanding of the coach's point of view, and (2) to model their negotiating after yours. If you feel uncomfortable taking this approach with your children, start by practicing with your spouse. Once you and your spouse feel comfortable, then try it with your children.

Once your children learn this "seek first to understand, then to be understood" principle, encourage them to negotiate with someone who maintains control over their access to future opportunities. They need the assurance that if they approach the situation in the proper manner, it will not backfire on them. But they also need to understand that to achieve high levels of excellence in anything, they need to take some risks and make tough decisions. For example, it may be necessary for them to temporarily give up a starting position on the team if they miss a practice or a game for another activity. However, as long as they have demonstrated that they understand the coach's position, and that the coach understands their position in advance of their absence, they should be able to feel confident that the costs to them will be minimal.

7

HELP YOUR CHILDREN LEAD BALANCED LIVES

Show your children the value of leading balanced lives.

Something about childhood and adolescence lends itself to obsession, as any parent who has lived through the "Barney," "Power Ranger," or "Leonardo DiCaprio" phenomena understands. Children and teenagers love to throw themselves wholeheartedly into their interests, and steering them into other pursuits can be challenging.

When that obsession is with sports, you may not see any harm in letting your children dedicate themselves to the life of an athlete. After all, sports is a wholesome, fun activity that benefits your children's physical and mental health and can even lead to college scholarships, perhaps even millions of dollars in professional contracts. And to be honest, what parents of an athletic child would not like to see their son or daughter's face on the cover of *Sports Illustrated*?

Remember, though, how easily you and your children can become obsessed with sports (both as a participant and a spectator), an obsession that may be harmful in many ways. First, even if a young athlete does manage to beat the odds and become a professional competitor, the athletic career rarely extends beyond the mid-30s. At an age when most people's careers begin to take off, the athletic career ends. This shock can be traumatic for athletes—especially those who have few, if any, other interests or activities to pursue.

Second, we have found that success in one area does not compensate for failure in others. For example, athletes with low grade-point averages can forget about college scholarships until they pull those grades up. Or people who throw themselves into sports while neglecting their interpersonal skills might find themselves unable to maintain successful relationships with others. What good is a wall full of trophies without someone to share them with?

Third, most experts agree that when you take the time to renew different aspects of your life, you strengthen the areas you are not working on as well. Weight trainers understand this principle. They know that they cannot work the same set of muscles every day. Muscles that get needed rest become stronger than ever.

Finally, we live in a rapidly changing world; most individuals will go through several careers in a lifetime. You can do much to prepare your children for the new millennium by helping them learn a wide range of skills that equip them to adapt to the changes they will face.

Of course, realize that your sermons on the benefits of leading a balanced life will only hit home if you model balance yourself. The father who works 70 hours a week and rarely attends a game and the mother who has no interests outside of her children both send negative messages. If you want the best for yourself and your children, implement and model the rules of balance in your own life.

8

HELP YOUR CHILDREN ASSESS THEIR INTERESTS

Encourage your children to experiment with a variety
of sports and to regularly assess the impact of
sports experiences on their lives.

Ultimately, children should be the ones to decide how
much time or energy they want to invest in sports. It is your job,
however, to insist that your children enjoy a wide range of sports
experiences. Often, ambitious coaches and parents place
considerable pressure on gifted athletes to specialize in a particular sport. Resist the temptation to foster early specialization. That way, you give your children time to accumulate
experience upon which to base their own decisions.

For some children, specialization is never the right decision. Take Kristin Folkl, for example. Kristin is the former
Stanford University volleyball and basketball star who went on

to play on the USA national volleyball team *and* in the WNBA. Throughout her sports career, Kristin balanced the two sports and played them at a world-class level without compromising either her academic or social life.

How can you help your children make decisions about how much and what kind of specialization is right for them? The first step is to listen carefully to what your children say about their experiences with sports. It may sound easy, but it takes a little practice to become effective. Concentrate on hearing what your children are saying, not what you *want* them to be telling you.

Secondly, become an astute observer of how your children choose to use their time. For example, do they spend all their free time in the driveway shooting hoops, or do they spread their time among several sports?

Third, if your children want to take sports seriously, encourage them to seek an assessment of their athletic abilities from an impartial and knowledgeable third party. Most importantly, though, schedule regular meetings with your children to review and evaluate their sports experiences and discuss how these experiences might affect any sports decisions that need to be made.

During these review sessions you will be tempted to make the assessments for your children based upon your superior knowledge and experience. Keep in mind that if you give in to these temptations, you (1) lose credibility with your children, and (2) lose a precious opportunity to help them learn an important part of the decision-making process. So even when you feel your children's assessment is wrong (*e.g.*, your daughter decides to specialize in softball when you feel she is more suited for basketball), let your children make mistakes. Learning from these mistakes will teach your children much more than you can ever teach by denying them the opportunity to try.

9

TEACH YOUR CHILDREN TO MAKE INFORMED DECISIONS

Help your children develop the skills they need to make informed choices as they move through their sports careers.

As children progress through the sports system, they face numerous decisions about which sports to try, which ones to specialize in, what college to choose, and so on. While the answers to these questions vary from athlete to athlete and from family to family, the basic principles involved in making these decisions remain the same.

First, your child, not you—should be the primary informa-tion-gatherer. When your child actively participates in gathering information, he or she is in a good position not only to make better choices, but also to assume "ownership" for the decision. Offer helpful suggestions about how to gather information ("You know, it might be helpful to talk to someone who's been to that camp and see what they thought of it"), but avoid being the one who writes to colleges or brings home stacks of books on soccer, lacrosse or whatever.

Second, make yourself available as a sounding board for your children during the decision-making process. Help your children assess the pros and cons of possible decisions. To succeed, avoid saying, "I think"; instead, ask your child, "What do *you* think?" or "How would *you* feel about that?"

After finishing the appropriate research and debating the merits of various decisions, empower your child to make the final decision about how (or whether) to take advantage of a sports opportunity. Granted, sometimes you will need to step in and make that decision—such as when financial constraints make it impossible for a child to attend a special sports camp—but for the most part, you should allow your children to make their own decisions, even if you disagree with them. This process of making decisions and living with the consequences helps us mature and develop as human beings.

10

HELP YOUR CHILDREN DEAL WITH ADVERSITY

Prepare your children for the injuries and psychological
hurts that athletes inevitably experience.

In sports, it is impossible to avoid pain, frustration, disappointment, or abuse from opponents and spectators. That is
why we do our children a disservice if we fail to prepare them
for these situations. How to prepare them is the question.

Two schools of thought conflict over how best to prepare
children for the inevitable setbacks they will face in sports, and
for that matter, in life itself. One school of thought (we will call it
the "Marine Corps Method") says the best way to prepare people
for stressful, difficult experiences is to give them practice in
being challenged and stressed. In sports, this approach is
known as "no pain-no gain" training. In other words, coaches

prepare their athletes for "battle" by subjecting them to punishing practice drills and, sometimes, psychological harassment. The idea is what does not break the athletes makes them stronger.

The second school of thought (the "You can do it!" method) begins with the assumption that athletes with high self-esteem will face adversity better; thus, the goal is to encourage athletes to develop their skills to the point where they feel confident in any situation. When people have high levels of confidence in their abilities, they more capably block out distractions—like an opponent's taunting, an opposing crowd's boos, or even physical pain.

Coaches (and parents) who employ the "You can do it!" method provide athletes with regular opportunities to build confidence in a supportive environment. Athletes have more confidence when they know they can count on their coach to support them whether or not they execute on each and every play.

When preparing your children to deal with adversity, exercise care in how you respond when your child is hurt or makes an error on an important play. Two types of typical responses are actually counterproductive. The first is to ignore your child's pain or frustration. You need to "be there" for a child experiencing physical or psychological pain. "Being there" does not mean running out onto the field if your child gets a scrape; it means protecting the child from enduring hurt, the pain that lingers after the immediate physical or psychological injury. The second counterproductive response is experiencing every setback your child encounters as if it is happening to you.

Remember that sports is a percentage activity; the best batters get a hit every third time at bat, and the best field-goal percentages in basketball rate only slightly over 50 percent. If you become anxious over each failure on the playing field, your children's sense of that anxiety interferes with their ability to perform and their enjoyment of the game.

Perhaps you feel as though you are caught between a rock and a hard place: "Am I being too soft? Too hard?" Our advice is to err on the side of softness. At the same time, assure your children that setbacks are part of sports, and show your children you have confidence that they will succeed.

PART 2

Study Your Map

ACHIEVING SELF-AWARENESS THROUGH SPORTS

Youth sports provide your family with opportunities to
learn about itself — about the nature of your family
values and priorities, and how your perspectives on
sports and life impact your relationships with each other.

Your ability to enjoy your children's sports activities
and your readiness to make the most of your family's shared
sports experiences are influenced by your understanding of
how your own childhood sports experiences have affected you.
In this section, we invite you to "study your map," that is, to
determine whether the type of sports-parenting role you have
chosen for yourself is indeed getting you and your children
where you want to go. We help you understand how your

identity as a sports parent is shaped by your personal sports experiences; your sports knowledge level; your capacity for managing the frustration that often comes with the sports-parenting role; and your readiness to experiment with new approaches to sports. It is a fascinating journey of self-discovery from which all members of your family can learn and grow.

Principles For Studying Your Map

11

ASSESS YOUR KNOWLEDGE OF YOUR CHILDREN'S SPORTS

To become a contributing member of the youth sports community, you need to learn more about the games your children play.

We find it fascinating that two of the most common complaints we hear from coaches concern parents at opposite ends of the sports knowledge continuum. At one end are parents who are so knowledgeable that they continually provide instruction to their children, instruction that frequently contradicts—or at least falls short of reinforcing—what the coach is teaching. At the other end are parents who lack a clear understanding of the game and its rules. The common

element of both cases—and what many parents never realize—is that the children recognize the distance between their
coaches and parents, making the sport something that sepa-
rates the child from the family, not something that brings it
together. To make the sports experience something that you
and your children may enjoy as a family, avoid falling into one
of these categories.

Let us begin with the most knowledgeable dads and moms.
Your genuine interest in your children's sports is critical, but
you must also show them respect. Show them you believe they
know something, too.

If your interest in a sport comes through regular instruction
about how to improve, you risk dampening your child's interest
in the sport, regardless of your good intentions. No matter how
much you know about a sport, resist the temptation to take this
role. If your child asks you for help, by all means provide suggestions (just be careful to avoid contradicting the coach, which
leaves your child in the middle between wanting to please you
and wanting to please the coach). If not, leave the coaching to
the coach. Follow the approach of wanting to learn the sport
with your child; make that sport a common ground that strength-
ens family bonds. Even if you have played and watched a sport
for years, you can always learn something new.

Just as parents who know a lot about a sport sometimes
have trouble finding the best way to support their children's
sports involvement, so do parents who know very little. Under-

standably, you may find difficulty in getting very involved in a sport you do not understand. Unfortunately, your children may interpret your lack of involvement as a lack of interest in something that is an important part of their lives. If you want to reap the full advantages of your investment in youth sports, you need to become genuine partners with your children in learning about their sports.

We understand that you may struggle to find the time to learn more about your children's sports. You do your best to fulfill your responsibility by buying the uniform, getting your child to practice on time, and showing up for games. From your child's point of view, your willingness to open the checkbook and pop for an $85 pair of shoes is great, but becoming positive sports parents involves something different. What your children really want are your two most precious commodities: time and attention.

Making the effort to learn more will pay off in several important ways. First, knowing more about a sport will make your children's competitions and practices more fun for you. Second, your sincere effort to learn more about a sport provides your children with a good model. And third, your children's confidence in your keen interest in their chosen sport encourages them to seek your counsel when they face uncertainty.

12

REVISIT YOUR CHILDHOOD SPORTS EXPERIENCES

Reviewing your childhood experiences and feelings
about sports can help you avoid imposing your
attitudes and beliefs about sports on your children.

Like it or not, your own childhood sports experiences
will likely affect the way you respond to your children's interest,
or lack of interest, in sports. Take some time to review your
personal history with sports. Without much difficulty, most of
you will recall the highs and lows of childhood athletic competitions. Your first home run or the time you fell off the balance
beam and broke your arm are moments not easily forgotten.
Might these experiences affect how you feel about your child
wanting to try out for baseball or gymnastics?

Before you answer, we want to emphasize that a person's attitudes are more complex than this. It is not enough simply to remember what sports you played, which teams you beat. Also ask yourself such questions as these: How did I feel about my coaches and teammates? Were my parents supportive of my involvement in sports? Did I appreciate their support? How did my family, friends, and coaches impact my feelings about sports? What values did my parents and coaches emphasize? Did they emphasize winning or having fun? Did my parents focus on my individual performance or the team? How did my parents handle my sports setbacks? What were the rides home with my parents like after a win or a loss?

While you think of answers to these questions, also think about your current sports involvement. Are you an athlete, coach, or referee? If so, ask yourself how that impacts your relationships with your children's sports. Does the time you spend enjoying your own sports have a positive or negative impact on your children?

Developing insight into the roots of your own perspective on sports will help you control any of your own attitudes and beliefs about sports that might damage your children's abilities to enjoy sports and/or to shape their own sports careers.

13

LOOK AT SPORTS THROUGH YOUR CHILDREN'S EYES

*To better understand your children's viewpoints,
learn to set aside your own feelings about sports.*

Before we can expect someone to understand our point of view, we must first try to understand theirs. This principle is true in all aspects of life—sports included. It is natural that we want to share our wisdom with our children in hope that they will avoid our most painful mistakes. However, as parents we sometimes forget that the advice we give our children ("You've got to be more aggressive on the court, Ty!" "Boys don't like it when a girl beats them all the time, Lisa") is influenced by our own sports history and values. It does not necessarily, nor for that matter should it, reflect how our children feel about sports.

Because sports exist in very rule-bound, cut-and-dried arenas, we sometimes fail to realize that people view them in different ways. Adults, especially, tend to see sports as competition and winning, whereas children (especially younger ones) more often see sports as fun and play.

To avoid indoctrinating children, and to encourage genuine exchanges with them about sports, try to do two things: 1) Become more aware of your personal values, along with how you communicate them; and 2) Learn how to ask genuine, not probing or leading, questions that encourage heartfelt responses from your children.

If you recognize the origins of your beliefs and think before you initiate conversations about sports with your children, your children will be more likely to develop their own unique perspectives on sports.

Make the effort to understand your children's perspective. Getting "into their heads" is more difficult than you might think. Asking questions is not enough. When parents ask questions, children sometimes suspect that they are being set up for criticism or unsolicited advice. Asking questions is important, but you must take care to ask the right questions at the right time.

For example, never discuss your child's perspectives on sports in the car on the way home from a competition. At that time, your athlete is more than likely mentally replaying the game and may be too caught up in emotions to think. Instead, take advantage of the occasional television or newspaper account of an athlete who has done something positive or negative. Share the article with your children and ask, "What do you think about this?"

Are we suggesting that you should avoid discussing your own sports values with your children? Absolutely not. Your children need to know what you believe and why. But avoid preaching or lecturing to your children about your sports beliefs. Doing so will limit your children's growth and interest in sharing ideas. By developing the skill to ask questions that result in thoughtful rather than defensive responses, you will gain a better understanding of your children, and they will become more receptive to and understanding of you.

14

LEARN TO COPE WITH FRUSTRATION

Take steps to deal with the inevitable frustration
that comes from getting involved in your
children's sports programs.

All parents feel a certain amount of frustration when
their child is performing on the playing field. After all, you have
little or no control over your child's actions during the game;
you have virtually no control over the coach's behavior; and
you have no control over how the game will turn out. This lack
of control is what frustration and anxiety are made of!

However, giving in to frustration on a regular basis will
ultimately harm you, your child, the rest of the family, and even
the youth sports team. Thus, you must take steps to reduce

your level of frustration before it takes the fun out of sports for everyone.

The first step is to recognize that frustration is inevitable, that everyone experiences it, and that it is not "caused" by your children's behavior. We are responsible for our own feelings of frustration—no one can make us feel frustrated unless we choose to. This means we can also choose not to feel frustrated. That power lies within us.

The trick is to recognize that things that frustrate us generally fall into two categories: things we can control and things we cannot control. If you think about it, the things that we can control tend not to frustrate us very long. Why not? Because we take whatever action we need to take, and the frustration disappears. If the television is too quiet, we turn it up. If the muffler on the car gets too loud, we get it fixed. On the other hand, things that lie beyond our control are the things that tend to frustrate us for a long time. Think about it for a moment. If something is beyond your control, what can you do? When you take the time to think about it, you will realize that the frustration really comes from having no ability to take action yourself. Instead, you have conversations with your family or friends—or even in your own head—in which you convince the other person to do something about it. The key to ending these frustrations is to recognize when you have no control over the situation. If you have no control, no amount of effort will make a difference. When such frustration strikes, remember how little

control you have, then move on to things that you can affect
yourself.

The next step is to develop the capacity to enjoy the full
range of pleasures that youth sports offer. Focusing exclusively
on whether your team is winning or your children are scoring
interferes with the simple joy of watching your children play.
Learn to take pleasure in such things as

- The growth of your children and their teammates;
- The grace of the athletes as they execute their skills;
- The camaraderie the athletes display;
- The way the athletes successfully deal with setbacks; and
- The fun of hanging out with other parents.

One of the best strategies for controlling frustration and
making youth sports an enjoyable experience for the entire family is to "adopt" all of your children's teammates and take responsibility for encouraging and supporting them as they work
to master the sport. You can even take this "adoption" concept
one step further and join with other team parents to develop a
mutually supportive extended sports family. Some of the best
performing teams we have witnessed over the years have been
those in which team families have formed a supportive clan
that protects everyone's interests, including the coaches'. You
will have an easier time accepting your children's setbacks when
you know that other parents are pulling for your children, too.

Creating a parent community with an upbeat, "You can do it" attitude is one of the best gifts you can give your children, the coach, the team, and yourself. Not only will you reduce your frustration level, but you will also increase the "joy level" of your youth sports experience.

15

DISCOVER NEW PERSPECTIVES ON SPORTS

Evaluate a variety of perspectives on sports to
determine which best suits your family's needs.

The great thing about sports in America is that they
serve as a way of building a common ground among diverse
people. The not-so-great thing is that within sports themselves
there is very little diversity, or room for different perspectives
on training, competing, winning, and losing.

Traditionally, sports have been based upon a win-lose model
where one person's gain is another person's loss. Competition
is often compared to a war and the winners to conquerors.
Athletes are frequently heard to say (after a particularly error-
prone competition), "Well, it wasn't pretty, but it was a win." In
other words, the emphasis is on winning, not on doing well or
on making the event "pretty."

While most people acknowledge that sports do not have to be based upon the traditional way of competing, everywhere we turn the values that underlie this perspective are reinforced by our sports legends, myths, and language. However, there are other ways of viewing sports that can be more rewarding than the traditional conqueror model.

For example, we can think of competition as a relationship in which opponents are respectful and caring as they test their skill against one another. Competition can be thought of as a process in which winning, of course, matters, as well it should. But how one plays, what one learns, and how the family and the community benefit by sports matter, too.

A viewpoint that is gaining in popularity is the win-win model, where the goal is to make everyone a winner in one way or another. To this end, some youth leagues have eliminated keeping score, which can put too much emphasis on outcomes and not enough on the game itself. To the traditionalist this approach is a tough sell.

For families to gain the greatest benefits from sports, new perspectives on how to take full advantage of the games their children play must find expression. Unfortunately, when parents go against the grain and begin to call for new avenues of enjoyment in youth sports, they frequently encounter considerable resistance from coaches, other parents, and even their own children. This common response reveals a natural resistance to change, even when change is being sought. What it comes down to is that parents who want to get the most out of their investment in sports need to stick to their guns and continue their search for better ways to be inspired and enriched by their family's experiences in youth sports.

Point the Way

HELPING YOUR CHILDREN USE SPORTS TO LEARN LIFE'S LESSONS

Sports provide you with opportunities to mentor your children as they face choices about how to use their sports experiences to grow and mature as human beings.

The most memorable learning experiences do not come from lectures and lessons. They are more a result of spontaneous insights—the right people in the right place at the right time. Sports are full of such teaching moments—most of them unanticipated, and many of them overlooked.

It is up to you to prepare yourself to take advantage of the teaching moments that will present themselves throughout your children's sports careers. This section is aimed at preparing you for some of the "life lessons" your children can learn as they play sports. It is designed to equip you to become the type of confidant that your children will seek out to guide them through this ever-changing, ever-complicated world.

Principles for Pointing the Way

16

HELP YOUR CHILDREN OVERCOME GENDER-ROLE STEREOTYPES IN SPORTS

Help your children understand that participating in sports does not make them any more or less masculine or feminine.

Traditionally, sports have been places where boys have learned to become men and girls have learned to cheer on the men in their lives. Today, almost everyone recognizes (intellectually, at least) that "real men" do not have to be jocks, and that girls who like to mix it up on the playing field are no less feminine than those who cheer their teams on from the sidelines.

But even though there have been radical shifts in our definitions of what constitutes appropriate behavior for men and women in recent years, many still believe that boys should be tough and girls should be tender. Held by coaches and others who guide and influence young athletes, these beliefs can profoundly undercut parental efforts to broaden the boundaries of their children's conceptions of manhood and womanhood. As parents, you face a real challenge to help your children break out of traditional male and female stereotypes. But we believe challenges are made to be overcome, and there are things that you can do to use sports as a tool for helping your sons and daughters expand their sense of what it means to be male or female.

The first and most effective step in supporting children as they clarify who they are is for you to model the patterns of behavior you want your children to emulate. Doing so is sometimes easier said than done. Even those couples who are committed to an equal partnership often find themselves unconsciously falling into patterns set by their parents and grandparents. In other words, while boys can learn to sew and girls can learn to repair the car, and boys can babysit and girls can mow lawns, parents seldom encourage such role reversals. Take advantage of these and other opportunities to help your children liberate themselves from traditional stereotypes. Take advantage of these opportunities to tell your children it is okay to chart their own paths.

You can also communicate your expectations to your children by celebrating the achievements of the men and women you admire who have broken gender stereotypes, both in and out of sports. And when daughters come home with tales of being made fun of by the boys because of their involvement in sports, or when sons make degrading remarks about "girl jocks," let your actions and words show you do not support such conduct.

Finally, when your family thinks about the values you wish to support through sports, put equal treatment for boys and girls on the agenda, then review that agenda from time to time to keep the issue high on your family's list of priorities. This way, you and your children can work together to develop new patterns of relating to one another as males and females. Sports can become settings for challenging these stereotypes.

Hopefully, the day will come when the whole world will emulate the TV commercial that has WNBA star Cynthia Cooper shouting to a couple of playground players, "Hey, you're playing like a couple of girls." They turn to her in anger, but upon recognizing her, their faces light up as they respond in unison, "Thanks." You have the power to hasten the coming of that day by supporting your daughter's sports dreams and helping your sons appreciate the qualities that women bring to sports.

17

HELP YOUR CHILDREN DEAL WITH AN OVERLY ZEALOUS COACH

Equip your children with strategies for responding to a coach who employs tough training methods.

Vince Lombardi. Bobby Knight. Bela Karolyi. All are legendary coaches and have consistently produced winners. All have used tough training methods and have reputations for being both demanding and insensitive to the emotional impact they may have on their athletes. While some athletes seem to thrive under the "tough love" approach to coaching, many do not. In fact, this style of coaching often has a negative impact on children and runs counter to the values underlying positive sports parenting.

Unfortunately, the success that these high-profile coaches have enjoyed means this hard-nosed approach is unlikely to go away. Therefore, since it is highly likely than an athlete will experience a "command and control" coach at least once during his or her career, it is important that you prepare to help your children deal effectively with this situation.

The first thing to do is to take your child's concerns about a coach's tough training methods seriously. Dads (who have often survived the same kind of treatment as young athletes) have a tendency to argue that a little toughness never hurt anyone and that their kids just need to "suck it up." Mothers, on the other hand, generally have not experienced this kind of coaching style, do not appreciate it in the least, and are ready to pull their child out of a tough program without further ado.

Before taking any action, get a detailed report from your children about what is happening. Also consider asking to attend a practice session so you can witness the coaching style first hand. If you conclude that the coach's style is not a good fit, either with the temperament of your child or your family's values, then talk to your child about what alternatives appear most attractive.

The first step in addressing the situation is to talk with your child about the situation and outline different approaches for holding a conference with the coach. If your child feels confident enough to approach the coach one on one, be supportive. Some children do not want their parents to step in too soon. However, avoid demanding that your child hold a one on one conference before you get involved. A truly hard-nosed coach might try to belittle your child, making her or him feel inadequate for even raising the possibility that the coach's style is not working with the child. In that case, express your willingness to go with your child to schedule a personal conference with the coach. In either case, it is important that someone approach the coach before any other action is taken. Sometimes different people see a situation differently, and this situation provides a good opportunity for both your child and the coach to be more effective in the future. Before this conference, regardless of whether you will be attending or not, prepare your child to take the lead and to talk to the coach in a non-combative, yet assertive, way. Emphasize that your child should do the talking, should be respectful and not criticize, but also emphasize that a belligerent reaction from the coach should not be tolerated. Tell your child that she or he has every right to leave—calmly—if the coach acts inappropriately. But help your child understand the difference between words that he or she would rather not hear and those that are really out of line.

If your child chose to meet with the coach one-on-one, but it did not work, with your child's permission, you may wish to talk to the coach about how your child is responding to the coach's style. It is important to underscore that the focus of this meeting is on the way the child is experiencing the coaching methods, not on the coaching style or on the personality of the coach. If this meeting fails to resolve the issue, you may choose to approach the program administrator. If no change occurs, and you conclude that the coach's style is genuinely diminishing your child's and other participants' spirits, then you may wish to mobilize other concerned parents to express concerns as a group to the coach, the administrator, and/or the persons to whom they report.

On the other hand, you may conclude after reviewing the situation that the coach's behavior is not extreme and no one is being injured by the techniques he or she is employing. In that case, you must decide whether to encourage your children to use the experience as a way of adapting to different coaching styles. The bottom line is that the decision needs to be your child's. Only the athletes themselves can decide if the coach is providing an experience that they are willing to endure in order to realize their sports dreams.

18

HELP YOUR CHILDREN ACHIEVE A BALANCE BETWEEN BEING SUCCESSFUL AND BEING A GOOD FRIEND

Use as teaching moments the inevitable frustrations that children face when choosing between an activity that results in being applauded or one that results in being liked and included.

Most children want to be the best at whatever they do—the smartest student, the most talented artist, the fastest runner. And most children seek to be liked, to be included in a group. Sports can be places where children can satisfy both of these needs. Through sports, children can develop their skills to a level that will bring them recognition for their achievements as athletes. They may also establish close relationships with their teammates, their family, and their community.

However, young athletes often find that their needs for being a success and for belonging conflict with each other. These situations present your children with powerful teaching moments.

Children of all ages are often more interested in talking to each other or "horsing around" during practices than in paying close attention to the coach. The young athlete's interest in building and maintaining relationships with teammates is frequently frustrating to coaches (and to their parents in the bleachers as well). We adults frequently find it difficult to understand why our children pass up excellent opportunities for furthering their skills. The importance of social life often becomes most apparent when your children bring the senior year in high school to a close. Often referred to as "senioritis," this condition manifests itself when athletes, who are caught up in the celebrations surrounding graduation, have difficulty focusing on their sports—or other activities.

At the opposite extreme are those athletes who get so wrapped up in the game and so preoccupied with their own success that they become totally insensitive to how they relate to those around them. Coaches may love these highly focused athletes, but they unfortunately often fail to develop the capacity for getting close to anyone in their lives.

Your children need to learn sooner, rather than later, that to live a full life requires not only the ability to be a success, but also the ability to establish intimate relationships with others.

Sports provide an ideal place in which to learn to achieve that balance. To succeed requires an effort on the part of both you and your athletic children.

Your role is to help your children cope with their feelings when the coach calls a practice for the same day that their friends have planned a social outing. Be available to help your children sort out the factors they should consider in making their choices. Avoid falling into the trap of making the decision for your children. Young athletes sometimes turn to parents to get them off the hook, either with their coach or their friends. Allowing yourself to get sucked into making a choice for your children relieves them from assuming responsibility for making the decision. Most importantly, it denies them an opportunity to develop their capacity to learn to live with the consequences of their actions.

Finally, help your children understand that "balance" does not necessarily mean everyone is always happy or satisfied with their decisions. Sometimes athletes will find that sports need to come first, even at the risk of compromising their social relationships. At other times, they will find that sports need to take a back seat. The key is to make sure that neither the investment in becoming successful on the playing field nor the investment in building a strong social network becomes an obsession for your children. To live full and satisfying lives in their families and communities, everyone, young and old, needs a balanced portfolio.

19

HELP YOUR CHILDREN CONTROL THEIR TEMPERS

Help your children understand the consequences
of losing their tempers and develop strategies
for staying in control.

Successful "players" in all walks of life are those people
who realize they have the power to take control of their lives.
They understand that self-control is the key to both mental and
physical health and that it contributes enormously to their overall
well-being. Individuals who exercise self-control also generally have higher self-esteem than those who do not.

Unfortunately, sports and self-control do not always go
together. For one, sports generate strong emotions. In addition, athletes, trained to be aggressive competitors, may have
trouble turning that aggression off. The fact that athletes often
receive special treatment from peers, teachers, family members, and others can also lead them to believe that they can

get away with losing their tempers. You can do several things to help your children stay calm, cool, and collected. First, help your children understand the consequences of their behavior. Children need to realize that their loss of control affects others as well as themselves. In basketball, for example, a player who loses his or her temper can receive a foul or be ejected from the game (either way, both the team and athlete are punished). If the behavior is bad enough, the player could be suspended from the team.

Parents must also enforce their own standards of behavior on their athletic children. Just because the coach might allow athletes to get away with certain kinds of behavior does not mean parents have to put up with it. (Our favorite example is the father who became so upset at his son's outbursts on the tennis court that he marched out and took the boy's racket away. When the young man whined, "But, Dad, I can win this game!" the father replied, "I don't see how. You don't have a racket.") While we do not endorse punishing children publicly, we do feel that parents must exercise leadership by setting and enforcing standards of sportsmanship.

Another thing you can do is help your children understand the "why" behind their loss of control. For example, if children always get angry when corrected by a coach, is it because they feel inferior? Do they feel like they are under pressure to always be perfect? Also, are there predictable times when they lose control—such as when they are over tired or in the middle of a stressful game? When children become more aware of when they are going to lose control, they find it easier to do something about it.

Next, you can help your children think of effective intervention techniques that allow them to control their tempers. Such techniques might include counting to ten, taking a deep breath, pounding their fist into their hand, or even thinking of a special "nonsense" word to say (instead of more offensive language).

Finally, and most importantly, reinforce positive behavior by catching your children being under control, rewarding them for being able to successfully manage their emotions. Also, every time you help your children feel good about themselves, you contribute to the development of the confidence your children need to remain under control. Remaining under control contributes to your children's confidence, and being confident contributes to being under control. It is a two-way street. You occupy a unique position to impact both your children's self-esteem and their ability to gain control over their emotions.

20

HELP YOUR CHILDREN REALISTICALLY ASSESS THEIR OWN PERFORMANCES

Learn ways to objectively evaluate your children's performances.

Because sports are very competitive and measurement-oriented, children often measure themselves against the skills and accomplishments of others or against their own high standards. When they employ unrealistic standards, though, they may feel inadequate. The challenge for you is to help your children learn how to realistically assess their performances.

There are several ways to accomplish this goal. One way is to encourage young athletes to seek out individuals who are knowledgeable in the sport and who are available to give them objective feedback. Children generally accept advice and criticism best from impartial outsiders, as opposed to their parents or siblings.

Also encourage your children to measure their performances against themselves, not against others. To do so objectively, teach your children the basics of conducting a performance appraisal. Periodic performance appraisals are a good way for children to both set and recognize the achievement of goals or standards. They can help children feel good about themselves as well as recognize areas where they need to stretch or work harder.

Perhaps the hardest thing for parents to do is to refrain from giving unasked-for opinions and advice. We encourage you to have open dialogues with your children, to ask for their comments and opinions, and to WAIT for your children to do the same. Once your opinion is requested, keep your comments positive. Above all, remind your children that sports are about learning and enjoying, not about being voted "Most Valuable Player" or making it to the pros.

21

HELP YOUR CHILDREN TAKE RESPONSIBILITY FOR SETBACKS

Teach your children the importance of taking responsibility for and working to overcome setbacks.

After a particularly physical basketball game between the Miami Heat and the Utah Jazz, in which Utah's Karl Malone took quite a beating, an interviewer asked Malone if he felt frustrated by all the fouls the referees were not calling. Malone just smiled and rolled his eyes. When he did answer, he brought up two important points: one, that you could not let the referee's actions affect your game; and two, the no-calls would not have had as big an effect if Karl had been playing up to his potential, which he had not been doing for several games.

The best athletes—and Malone is certainly one—understand the importance of taking responsibility for their actions, good or bad. They avoid wasting their energy trying to blame others for things that go wrong in their lives. Rather, they concentrate on solving the problems that lie in front of them so they can move on to other things. They are proactive. Proactive individuals realize that they have the ability to choose how they will react to circumstances. Reactive people, on the other hand, let outside factors—the weather, a bad call by a ref, a critical comment from their coach—influence how they feel and what they do.

Accepting responsibility is difficult, no matter what your age. While accompanying her three-year-old son to the dentist, one woman was surprised to hear the dentist playfully chiding his assistant about a piece of equipment. "You're supposed to say, 'I broke it, and I take responsibility,'" the dentist said. Noting the puzzled look on the face of his patient's mother, the dentist explained that the subject of that week's staff meeting had been "personal responsibility." "Gee," the woman said, looking at her little boy, "you mean I have to keep teaching him that lesson all of his life?"

Help your children understand that accepting responsibility puts them in a position of power. Instead of being at the mercy of things they have no control over, they have the power to choose how they will react in any given situation, regardless of what teammates, coaches, or referees may do. In other words, it is not what happens to you that matters; it is what you do about it that makes the difference.

Sports provide many opportunities for your children to make mistakes and therefore to make excuses for the setbacks they experience. All young athletes feel a great temptation to refuse responsibility for their actions. However, rather than simply sharing your child's disappointment, it is essential that you approach their setbacks as providing opportunities to teach them to assume responsibility for their actions and to develop the resolve to overcome the setbacks they experience. While it is important to acknowledge the pain and frustration your children experience at the time of the setback, it is equally important to take the occasion of their frustration to help them develop the capacity to bounce back. Both in sports and in life the ability to recover from setbacks is what makes the difference between those who take charge of their lives and those who let circumstances take charge of them. Go beyond empathy and provide encouragement for your children "to get back on the horse" that has just bucked them off. Unlike many life situations, sports nearly always allow athletes opportunities to sharpen their skills so that they achieve greater mastery. Your task is to encourage them to take full advantage of these second chances.

22

TEACH YOUR CHILDREN TIME-MANAGEMENT SKILLS

Help your children efficiently organize their time so that they keep up with their schoolwork and actively participate in family and community life.

Essentially, time management is self-management. That is one reason why people who fail to manage their time well often have problems with self-esteem—they know that it is not their time they cannot seem to manage; it is themselves.

Because sports participation requires a large investment of time, young athletes are especially vulnerable to feeling that there simply are not enough hours in the day for them to accomplish everything they want to do. It seems safe to conclude that in today's fast-paced world, there will always be time pressures. Children who learn to deal with these pressures while young will be that much better off when they become adults.

Probably the biggest hurdle you face in helping your children learn how to effectively manage their time is getting them to recognize the causes of their ineffective time management behavior. All the management strategies in the world will fail to help your children if they do not face up to what is preventing them from efficiently using their time.

Some common barriers to efficiently using time include

- Lack of written personal goals
- Disorganization (e.g., assignments are turned in late because they get buried in a pile on a desk)
- Over-commitment
- Procrastination
- Indecisiveness
- Fatigue
- Lack of self-discipline
- Interruptions (e.g., answering every phone call while trying to study)
- Unrealistic expectations
- Preoccupation with personal problems ("How can I concentrate on this paper after that stupid thing I said to Jackie today?")
- Inability to say "no"

To overcome these common barriers, your children must recognize which of these patterns of behavior are interfering with their ability to manage themselves so that they can integrate their sports activities into the rest of their lives without compromising the realization of their other dreams. In addition, it is valuable for you and your children to come to a better understanding of why they are locked into self-defeating patterns. Is it because they do not have the confidence in themselves that they fail to try to better organize their time? Is it because they are locked into a peer group that has come to govern their lives and draw them away from achieving their athletic, academic, family, and community goals? Is it because you as parents have difficulty managing your own time? Is it because your children lack the technical skills to put their lives in order, that is, that they do not know how to establish a list of goals and identify the behaviors needed to make progress toward these goals? You can help your child conduct this self-assessment.

The best way for your child to counter time-wasting patterns of behavior is to come to a greater awareness of their current way of doing things. Also, they need to achieve a better understanding of what is perpetuating these inefficient habits. And they need to be very clear about their priorities. You can help your children achieve better self-understanding as you assist them in setting priorities. By working with you to develop greater self-understanding, your children can learn to manage themselves and their time with greater effectiveness. This achievement will permit them to gain greater control over their lives, which will in turn lead them to feel better about themselves.

You will be most successful in helping your children manage the competing demands in their lives by working collaboratively with them in addressing their time-management problems. Nagging and preaching are unlikely to succeed. If you too have difficulty managing your time (and who among us does not) it could be useful to work alongside your children in putting more order into all of your lives. Modeling, of course, is one of the most effective ways for you to influence your children's behavior.

23

HELP YOUR CHILDREN MAKE SENSIBLE DECISIONS ABOUT TOBACCO, DRUGS, AND ALCOHOL

You are responsible for helping your children understand the impact of tobacco, drug, and alcohol use on their athletic performances and personal well-being.

It is ironic that athletes, who more than anyone should understand the need to stay physically and mentally fit, could ever have a problem with substance abuse. And yet we hear stories every day of young athletes getting kicked off the team for drug use or arrested for drunk driving. Why do they do it?

Anyone who watches sports on TV should not be surprised to find a close association between athletes and alcohol consumption. During the commercial breaks of nearly every sports broadcast there is a barrage of 30-second ads that closely associate sporting events with beer drinking: "It's refreshing." "No, it's the great taste." has become deeply ingrained in the minds of all regular sports viewers. And the Budweiser frogs and lizards have endeared themselves to sports fans throughout the nation. We have become so accustomed to these sometimes imaginative and entertaining creations that we have lost sight of the kind of message these ads send to our children. Likewise, the fact that we have legal prohibitions against underage drinking, by its very nature, sends the message that one way to be identified as an adult is start consuming alcohol.

In addition, we are also not always aware of how strongly alcohol consumption is related to our definitions of manhood in American culture. There is a generally accepted belief that "real men" not only love sports, but also have developed a hearty appetite for alcohol. Similarly, watching a baseball player chewing tobacco appears no more notable than watching him swing a bat. There is very little public uproar when an athlete or a coach is arrested for "driving while under the influence" of alcohol or drugs, especially if the athlete or coach is popular with the local fans. We seem to have concluded that "Boys will be boys, what do you expect?" Many sports families have become immune to reports of athletes who have abused alcohol and fail to make a "big thing" over these legal transgressions.

There are many other reasons why athletes are prone to abuse tobacco, alcohol, and drugs besides the general acceptance of alcohol as a tradition in the sports culture. The pressure to succeed and the need to recapture the "highs" of competition can lead an athlete to drug or alcohol abuse. Sometimes the confidence athletes need to be successful also leads them to believe they are immune to the addictions that afflict "lesser" mortals. For the top-level athlete, alcohol is a depressant that can be used to relax from the extreme pressures of the game. Baseball players say the same thing about chewing tobacco—it helps them relax.

No doubt the greatest pressures that push young athletes into tobacco, drug, and alcohol use comes from their peers. Studies show that drug use among teenagers, which declined during the 1980s, is increasing at an alarming rate while the perceived risk is decreasing. For example, a panel of teenagers convened by *USA Today* reported that marijuana use is now so widespread that most teens do not even consider it a drug.

What can you as sports parents do to counter this emerging pattern among young people? First, never assume that it could not happen to your children. You must begin talking with your children at an early age about the consequences—physical, emotional, legal—of using tobacco, drugs, or alcohol as a youth.

Second, do more than tell your children to "just say 'no.'" Saying "no" to something many of their peers are doing is very difficult, indeed. Kids need to know why they are saying no, and they need to know how to say it. You must give your children information and the skills they need to make positive choices for themselves. Point to respected athletes and others who abstain from tobacco, alcohol, and drugs as examples that your children can point to when they feel pressure from their peers.

Finally, enforce your role as guardians of your children's welfare. Doing so means being "uncool" enough to do things like setting and enforcing curfews and calling other parents to make sure that parties will be chaperoned and alcohol free. By taking such actions, you send a powerful message about the dangers of tobacco, drug, and alcohol use. Also, model sensible approaches to alcohol use. It does little good for parents to preach against teen drinking when they themselves are seen as an embodiment of the sports fans celebrated in TV and print beer ads. And finally, work hard to disassociate drinking from manhood and adulthood through everything you do. Real men and women do not need to drink to be accepted by their peers.

24

HELP YOUR CHILDREN AVOID EATING DISORDERS

To help your children avoid eating disorders, you must encourage and support healthy behaviors, as well as do your part to counter the popular narrow definitions of beauty that exist in the American culture.

Our national obsession with weight and appearance pushes many people toward developing an eating disorder. Eating disorders generally start at a young age (80 percent of ten-year-old girls claim to be on a diet) and are not limited strictly to females. Male athletes who are pushed to maintain low weight are also susceptible to the development of eating disorders.

What can you do to help your children avoid developing an eating disorder?

- Educate your children about basic differences in body types and the role genetics plays in determining the type of body they will have.

- Ask yourself if you are doing things (teasing, criticizing, and so on) that over-emphasize beauty and body shape.

- Learn about and discuss with your children the (a) dangers of trying to alter one's body shape through dieting; (b) the value of *moderate* exercise in building stamina and cardiovascular fitness; and (c) the importance of eating well-balanced meals three times per day.

- Be a good role model when it comes to sensible eating, exercise, and self-acceptance.

- Help your children understand the ways in which television, magazines, and other media promote slenderness.

- Be alert to any negative messages your children's coaches might be sending about weight or appearance, and be prepared to discuss the issue with the coach.

- Do not limit your children's caloric intake unless a physician requests that you do so for medical reasons.

- Do whatever you can to promote your children's self-esteem and self-respect. Ensuring that children have strong self-esteem is probably the best way to prevent eating disorders.

(This list is adapted from "10 Things Parents Can Do to Help Prevent Eating Disorders," by Dr. Michael Levine)

How can you recognize if one of your children has, in fact, developed an eating disorder? One of the clearest indications is when the child reveals that he or she has an unrealistic image of his or her own body. For example, if a young girl who has lost a significant amount of weight says, "I don't feel or look thin to myself at all," she is showing that she does not have a realistic view of her body. Any time you suspect an eating problem, you should immediately seek professional help. Your family doctor or pediatrician should be able to recommend a therapist who is well versed in treating eating disorders.

25

HELP YOUR CHILDREN SELECT GOOD ROLE MODELS

Be aware of who your children are choosing as role models and take actions to ensure that appropriate models are available.

When your sweet-faced son comes home and announces, "Dennis Rodman is so cool! I want to be like him when I grow up!" you might easily wonder where you have gone wrong. However, before uttering the phrase, "Over my dead body," take a deep breath and instead try something like this: "That's an interesting choice. What is it you admire so much about Dennis Rodman?" By taking this approach, you not only avoid passing judgment on your child's choice, but you also open the way for a meaningful dialogue about the difference between celebrities and role models.

The difference between a celebrity and a role model is important for your children to understand. When they choose an athlete as a role model, are they making that choice because the athlete has many qualities they admire, or because they have seen the person frequently in the media, causing them to conclude that it must be "cool" to get all that attention?

Sports fans often create myths about high-profile athletes, failing to acknowledge their shortcomings. But the most influential people in the lives of children are parents, brothers, sisters, neighbors, those people from whom they learn everyday behavior. Parents and their children need to understand that real role models are those people who teach them how to live their lives, and those are the people with whom they are most intimate.

Can celebrities be good role models? Certainly. There is nothing wrong with a child looking at Dennis Rodman and saying, "You know, he doesn't always do things that I agree with, but I admire the way he doesn't care if he's different from everyone else."

Of course, your children might need a little help from you to learn how to look beyond the surface of a celebrity to identify those skills and qualities worth emulating. How can you do so? Start by learning who your children's role models are and then research their lives. That way, when your child expresses admiration for someone like Mark McGwire, you may respond with, "Yes, it's amazing that he was able to hit all those home runs. But you know what I really like about him? The way he gives a lot of his money to help abused children. Now, that's something that really makes a difference in a person's life."

You can also help your children by making sure they have access to a variety of appropriate role models. Single mothers, for example, may turn to their children's grandfathers, uncles, or family friends to act as male role models.

Keep in mind, though, that your children's most important role models should be the people to whom they are the closest—you, their parents. When it comes to setting examples—including that of making sports a positive experience—you are on the front line. It may seem like a tremendous responsibility, and sometimes it is. But more often than not, being a role model consists of carrying out those small, daily acts of unnoticed courage and kindness that show your children how to live positive and content lives.

Take Care

CREATING A SUPPORTIVE SPORTS CLIMATE

Sports provide your family with opportunities and responsibilities for creating a climate that is uplifting and enriching for all participants.

There is much you can do as a parent to contribute to the creation of a positive climate in which your children, their teammates and coaches, and other team families can realize their sports dreams. This section focuses on how your family can work together to establish a foundation that allows everyone to benefit from their investment in sports. It includes discussions on making everyone a winner, understanding sibling rivalry, helping your children deal with problem coaches, encouraging sportsmanship, creating a family-friendly sports environment, and other issues that will help you create a positive sports climate that will pay off handsomely, both in the enjoyment your family will gain from your sports experiences and in the lessons you and your children can learn about yourselves and your sports compatriots.

Principles For Taking Care

26

MAKE EVERYONE A WINNER

You have many opportunities to help make sports a
renewing and empowering experience for everyone involved.

Sports do not need to be an activity where one person's
gain is another's loss. Granted, only one team is ahead on the
scoreboard when the game ends. But beyond points, assists,
yards gained, tackles, strikeouts, aces, birdies, kills, and goals,
many other factors contribute to a successful and enjoyable
sports experience. You do not have to sit by and allow either
tradition or the values of others to shape your family's sports
experiences. Instead, you have the opportunity to work with

your children, the coaches, and other parents to "rewrite" the score book.

Positive sports experiences occur most often when participants mind the details of the sports activity in progress. For example, uplifting and enjoyable sports moments can come from

- the beauty of the sports setting
- the drama of the competition
- displays of virtuosity, good form, or unique style
- an athlete's or a team's development
- shared symbols and traditions
- mutually supportive relationships
- pre- and post-game ceremonies
- band music and cheerleaders
- half-time hotdogs and soft drinks
- celebrations that occur when a "test" is completed.

Winning is an essential goal of a sports event, but when it becomes the primary focus for athletes, coaches, parents, and spectators, these other opportunities for enjoyment can be lost. To win a game, match, or championship is satisfying, but there are so many other sources of enrichment available that a significant loss occurs when the smaller pieces of the "sportscape" are ignored. By widening and deepening your focus, you can better observe and enjoy what is taking place around you and share that joy with your children and others in your extended sports "family."

27

ACCENTUATE THE POSITIVE

You can help raise sports to a higher level by
demonstrating a positive regard toward others
and celebrating all kinds of achievements.

A friend of ours, whose daughters participated in many
years of dance, shared this story about one of the dance
instructors:

"While my daughters were growing up, they attended the
same dance studio for many years and had a variety of teachers over the course of their training. Because parents were
allowed to come watch their daughters dance the first day of
every month, I soon became familiar with the different teachers and their teaching styles. One teacher never failed to
impress me. No matter how poorly a dancer performed, the

teacher would never give a criticism without first prefacing it with a positive remark. For example, a young girl who failed to keep her legs straight during her running leap might be told, 'Janie, you did a wonderful job of leaping high! Now let's try it again to see if you can get your legs a little bit straighter this time.' By the end of the year, every girl in this teacher's class would have walked over broken glass for her—and so would the parents." It was a wonderful example of looking for the positive first.

You, as a parent, perhaps more than anyone else, are in a position to raise sports to higher levels through your examples of positive behavior. What can you do to model respectful and caring behavior in the sports setting?

- Invite ideas and information from your children, the coaches, and the other parents, and listen carefully to what these individuals have to say.

- Show restraint by not imposing your own attitudes and beliefs on other sports participants.

- Include your children and the coaches in sports decision-making.

- Reward mutual support whenever it is displayed.

- Display an openness to others' ideas.

- Control potentially disruptive emotions.

- Express concern for other sports participants.

Above all, you model a positive approach to sports when you provide encouragement to your children and their teammates. To "en-courage" is basically to give your children the gift of courage. This helps your children take those risks that make sports a positive growing experience.

28

BE SENSITIVE TO SIBLING RIVALRY

Help your children develop mutually
supportive relationships.

Parents of two outstanding college basketball players
who played for different teams at the same time were once
asked how they handled it when their sons' teams competed
against each other. Their answer? "We just root for whoever
has the ball."

Sibling rivalry is an inevitable challenge in every family with
more than one child, especially when the children are close in
age. When your children choose to compete with each other, it
does not necessarily signal that you have failed. It simply
reveals a reality of family life. Positive sports parents will not
deny that their children are in competition with one another.
Instead, they will work to prevent this natural rivalry from

escalating into a situation where the esteem of one child is diminished by the perception that the parents care more about the other child's life.

Very seldom is athletic talent distributed equally among all the children in a family. This reality presents a real dilemma for parents. If you invest more in the most accomplished athlete, you risk making less-accomplished children feel as if they are less important than the family "star." On the other hand, if you attempt to compensate for the attention the star receives through sports, the star begins to ask, "What do I have to do to get my parents' respect and love?"

Besides recognizing sibling rivalry for what it is, make an effort to set aside time for each child's activities, whatever they may be. It is not necessary to maintain a time card to make sure that each child receives equal support. Just be sensitive to the ways that the non-stars relate to sports and be ready to develop and nurture their talents.

Also help your children develop mutually supportive relationships. Preaching to your children about responsibility to their siblings is unlikely to succeed. What does work is showing a genuine interest in the lives of each family member. When that happens, family bonds are naturally built and strengthened among siblings and parents.

29

HELP YOUR CHILDREN DEAL WITH A CONTROLLING COACH

You must not allow your family's values to be compromised by a coach's desire to exert control over your children's lives.

Some coaches choose to "adopt" their athletes for the duration of the season. Sometimes their motives for doing so are altruistic; for example, they feel that an athlete or group of athletes shows high promise, and the best way to get them to achieve their potential is to control as many factors in their lives as possible—including what they eat, when they sleep, when and where they study, and with whom they associate.

Other times, a coach's motives are more selfish. A coach may lack close relationships in his or her own life, so athletes fill the void. Or a coach may have an excessive need for power, which is reflected in a need to tightly control athletes.

Certainly, you want coaches to get the best performances from your children. You also like to have coaches take a special interest in your children's lives outside sports. But few of you wish to turn over your parenting functions to a coach. When coaches cross this line, you may be made to feel that you are irrelevant—only useful for feeding, clothing, and transporting your children.

To secure the welfare of your family, remain vigilant to patterns of coaching employed in your children's youth sports programs. When coaches refuse to allow you to attend practices or competitions, they raise a red flag. Just as in the case with a tough or overly zealous coach (Principle 17), you need to listen to your children when they come home with stories about the coach's conduct, attitudes, and values that run counter to family values. Listen carefully to assess the reports, then discuss with your children how they view their coach's actions.

Any time you and your children must deal with a coach who is less than a "perfect fit" for your family, several learning opportunities present themselves. First, you and your children may talk about what makes people tick, and why different individuals behave the way they do. Your children also have the opportunity to assess what they really want to get out of sports, and how much they are willing to sacrifice to achieve their goals. For example, if your children are mainly into sports for fun, they might prefer to find a different coach, or even quit a particular sport, rather than subject themselves to coaching techniques that make them uncomfortable. On the other hand, if your children hope to become elite athletes, they might choose instead to turn their lives over to a top coach who has the potential to help them achieve their dreams.

In those cases where your children choose to stay in a program with a controlling coach, the family needs to remain alert to signs that their sense of well-being and competency are intact. One of the biggest dangers of working with a controlling coach is the possibility that the children may come to believe that they are incapable of acting without the coach's input. To avoid this situation, help your children develop effective means of preserving their sense of competency and well-being, as well as their sense of commitment to your family and the values you embrace.

30

HELP YOUR CHILDREN DEAL WITH AN ABUSIVE COACH

Help your children recognize signs of verbal, physical, and sexual abuse by coaches.

Over the years numerous cases of verbal, physical, and sexual abuse by coaches have come to public attention. The evidence suggests that far too many children are being subjected to unprofessional conduct by coaches. The consequences for athletes can be tragic and have an enduring impact on their lives.

There is no doubt as to where you as parents stand in cases of sexual abuse. No parent wants a trusted adult to take sexual advantage of their child. The distressing thing about cases of sexual assault involving coaches is that, in many cases, children are not forcibly raped by a coach. Rather, a coach persuades the athlete that they have a special place in their coach's life. Young people are extremely vulnerable to advances from a coach and need to be aware of the consequences of entering into such relationships.

Physical abuse by coaches is harder to identify. Clearly, if a coach strikes a player (consider the notorious example of legendary football coach Woody Hayes), she or he leaves no doubt about exceeding professional boundaries. On the other hand, some coaches gain personal satisfaction from putting their athletes through grueling physical drills that test their limits. In these cases you may have trouble drawing the line between hard physical workouts for purposes of conditioning and those that step outside acceptable boundaries.

While the NCAA has imposed limits on the duration of training at the college level, no such rules prevail at the youth sports level. Signs of physical abuse that you can watch for include regular reports of excessive training, and/or a rash of injuries occurring among athletes on a team. Such injuries often signify over-training. At this point, you should observe the coach's training methods yourself and seek the counsel of an experienced sports training professional to determine whether your children are being put at risk.

Verbal abuse of athletes has become a staple of our national sports television diet. Who has not seen a college or professional coach screaming at a hapless athlete? Unfortunately, more and more coaches of young athletes emulate this high-profile behavior. Coaches justify their verbal tirades as essential to motivating today's athletes. Whether they are right is not the issue. If your family demands that family members demonstrate respect for one another, and at the same time your children's coaches model a verbally aggressive, disrespectful style, they violate your family code and send the wrong message to your children. When you know a coach is behaving in a way that is offensive to your family, then you and your children have every right to take appropriate action.

31

CONSULT YOUR FAMILY BEFORE COACHING YOUR CHILDREN'S TEAM

Before deciding to coach your children's team, you should discuss the issue with the family and carefully weigh the advantages and disadvantages.

Without volunteer moms and dads, youth sports in America could not survive. On the other hand, before you agree to coach your children's team, you should carefully consider how the responsibility will affect your entire family.

First, consider the impact on the child whose team you might coach. Children face a challenge to adjust to a parent who wears two hats: that of a nurturing, supportive parent and that of a demanding, evaluating coach. You may also have trouble maintaining objectivity about your own children. Sometimes you will feel tempted to give your child a break; other times you may demonstrate your "fairness" by giving more opportunities to other team members. Begin by determining if your parent-child relationship will allow both you and your child to move between these two roles without great difficulty. Many children have difficulty making the transition.

Second, consider the other children in your family. If you coach one child's team but not the other, you may aggravate natural sibling rivalry. Stay alert for evidence of jealously and rivalry, and make an effort to spend appropriate time with the child whose team you do not coach.

Third, consider your own needs. The coaching role denies you the opportunity to enjoy the camaraderie of the other parents on the sideline, which for many parents is one of the most enjoyable parts of participating in youth sports. You also face the pressure of dealing with the baggage that comes with coaching young athletes—irate parents, upset children, scheduling conflicts, and so on. These challenges require patience, a sense of humor, good communication skills, and above all, an enjoyment of working with children. Honestly ask yourself if you have these essential coaching qualities.

Finally, consider your spouse. Spouses get to experience many of the same stresses as their coaching partners, but without controls over outcomes and without as many of the rewards. Spouses also find themselves in the position of having to compete with youth sports for attention. For some spouses, this is not a great sacrifice; for others, it can become a major irritant.

If you are asked to coach your child's team, take some time to consider the full range of possible consequences. Since the decision impacts everyone in the family, place the issue on the agenda of a specially scheduled family meeting, and consider everyone's input.

32

CONSIDER THE PROS AND CONS OF TEACHING SPORTS SKILLS TO YOUR CHILDREN

Consult with the coach and your children before attempting to teach your children athletic skills.

No matter how "sports savvy" you are, teaching sports skills to your own child is tricky business. Even Roger Clemens—a five-time Cy Young winner with four sons—admitted on a television talk show that his boys would take baseball instruction from someone else before they would listen to him. "To them, I'm just 'Dad,'" he explained.

In many cases high-profile athletes have been successfully trained by parents, apparently without compromising their parenting relationship (Tiger Woods and Venus and Serena Williams come to mind). But in other cases this experience has led to disaster for both parent and child.

Before you take on the task of teaching an athletic skill to any of your children, consider the following:

- Does the child genuinely want you to be his or her mentor?
- Are you competent (and patient enough) to teach the skill?
- Can you avoid becoming another competitor of your children?
- How does the coach feel about having parents teach skills to their athletes? Does the coach really want parents to work with their children away from the coach's supervision?
- Is your main desire to help your child improve, or to show up the coach?
- How will the extra emphasis on athletic achievement affect the parent-child relationship?
- What impact will working with one child have on other children in the family?

When it comes to having their parents mentor them in sports, children nearly always feel conflict. On the one hand, they seek their parents' approval; on the other hand, they wish to establish their independence—which in many cases means automatically disagreeing with anything their parents say. The fact that you as parents have been the major boundary setters also makes it difficult for your children to receive corrective sports feedback from you. Many parents feel uncomfortable dealing with the inconsistency and rejection that may result from trying to mentor their own children in sports.

If you do decide to undertake the task of teaching sports skills to your child, we recommend that you do so with 1) the unequivocal consent of your child; 2) the blessing of the coach (and the willingness of the coach to let you know which skill techniques to promote); and 3) the consent of other siblings so they do not feel slighted by the attention given to their brother or sister.

33

CREATE AN ENVIRONMENT WHERE GOOD SPORTSMANSHIP PREVAILS

Encourage sportsmanship in your children and others by living good sportsmanship yourself.

Many years ago, before the onset of professional opportunities, sports seemed to revolve primarily around creating well-rounded men and women. People promoted sports as a way to teach loyalty and leadership, balancing mental activities with physical exertion.

However, as sports have become less amateur oriented, this focus often gets lost. Many of today's athletes seem more concerned with developing themselves as a product than as a person. Even the phrase "Be a good sport" has come to have a negative connotation.

Help your children understand that it is not wimpy or geeky to be a good sport. Rather, being a good sport shows that the athlete has the strength of character to do what is right.

Know, too, that preaching sportsmanship to your children will leave you short of your goals; you must model good sportsmanship yourself.

For parents, good sportsmanship means

- Respecting the judgment and integrity of game officials
- Recognizing and appreciating outstanding play by both teams
- Refraining from negative comments and cheers
- Being supportive of other parents and players
- Acting in a civil manner towards officials, coaches, parents, and players

For children, good sportsmanship means

- Treating teammates and opponents with respect
- Respecting the judgment and integrity of game officials
- Displaying appropriate conduct (not arguing, making offensive gestures, or "trash talking")
- Playing fairly

Above all, good sportsmanship means more than just playing by the rules. Sportsmanship is setting a high standard for behavior and sticking to it. It is an ongoing effort of hard work, courage, and dedication to live your life in sports according to the highest personal standards.

34

HELP MAKE SPORTS FUN, FESTIVE, AND FRIENDLY

Assume leadership in helping sports become a
sanctuary from the normal stresses of everyday
life, a place where a good time is had by all.

As the girls' basketball team at a small, rural high school in Washington advanced further and further in their league standings, a group of fathers (several of whom had been basketball teammates many years earlier at the same school) came up with a bold strategy for showing their support: They shaved their heads. As the dads sat together in the stands, their shiny, glowing pates shone like beacons of encouragement for their daughters. Today the hair has grown back (most of it, anyway), but for the girls, their fathers, and all the others who were a part of that season, the memories linger on.

One of the most important functions of youth sports is to provide families with a place where they can get away from the pressures of everyday life and just enjoy being with family and friends in a fun, festive, and friendly atmosphere, where they can celebrate their accomplishments and reaffirm their commitments to one another. You play a major role in creating this kind of climate. Some of the most adventuresome parents do things like shaving their heads, but you do not have to be extreme to demonstrate your commitment to creating a positive sports environment. You can help create a festive atmosphere when you

- Remind one another of the importance of letting your children enjoy the game without being distracted by over-zealous, intrusive parents on the sidelines.

- Guard against creating scenes (by challenging the officials, yelling criticisms at your kids or the coaches, or squabbling with other parents).

- Express your joy at being able to share the sports experience with your children and the other families.

- Make an effort to establish a supportive community of parents.

- Create a festive spirit by embellishing the field, pool, or gym with banners, flags, signs; wearing special clothing (team colors, T-shirts, silly hats, etc.); sharing food and beverages with other families on the sidelines (potlucks, barbecues, etc.); or organizing "milestone" gatherings where everyone is encouraged to celebrate the team's accomplishments and reaffirm their commitment to the team's goals.

Remember that sports do not have to reflect the ugliness that occurs beyond the playing field. When sports begin to duplicate the sordidness and stresses that sometimes accompany everyday life, they typically lose their power to renew the spirits of those who watch and play the games.

35

CREATE A FAMILY-FRIENDLY SPORTS PROGRAM

Make sure your family interests are considered when sports policies and practices are formulated.

Youth sports vary greatly on how hospitable they are to families. In some programs, parents take an active role in all aspects of the operation, from coaching and refereeing to raising funds and cleaning up after events.

However, a trend toward "professionalizing" youth sports seems to be growing. You may feel better able to enjoy your children's sports experiences when you do not have to worry about organizing car washes or practice schedules. You may also like the idea of enlisting experienced experts to work with your children. On the other hand, you may prefer a more hands-on involvement—you feel a sense of "ownership" toward the program available in no other way.

When you opt for having your children's sports programs run by "professionals," you do gain time and avoid effort and conflict. But often this process, which makes sports involvement more comfortable and convenient, comes at the expense of lost opportunities for building a cadre of sports parents who can contribute to the creation of an enriching climate in which the children and the community can grow and prosper.

As youth sports move more and more in the direction of employing paid coaches, referees, administrators, and fund raisers, they have a tendency to develop into baby-sitting services that all too frequently keep parents at arm's length. In situations where parents remain uninvolved in the day-to-day operation of the youth sports programs, program administrators may begin to resent what they view as parental intrusions onto their turf. Neither of these outcomes benefits athletes or their families.

Are we suggesting that all youth sports programs should be parent operated, or that those programs which have been "professionalized" are detrimental to children and their families? Certainly not. However, we believe that all youth sports programs should be family-friendly organizations where program policies and practices reflect family needs and interests. At the very least, program administrators should regularly seek your input. Responsible program administrators make a habit of involving parents and mobilizing your support for their programs. Likewise, positive sports parents take full advantage of opportunities to imprint their children's sports programs with their ideas, values, and efforts.

Certainly, it is often difficult to address the needs of all families through a single sports program. However, the most successful programs in meeting family needs tend to be those in which the program heads regularly solicit and pay careful attention to what parents believe a youth sports program should do for their children, their families, and their communities.

36

INVEST IN FORMING AN INSPIRING SPORTS COMMUNITY

Help create a sports environment where participants
feel deeply involved in what they do and
feel closely connected to others.

A friend of ours once knew a young man in college who was enthralled with the movie *Star Wars*. He had seen the movie countless times, had smuggled a tape recorder into the theater to record the dialogue (this was in the pre-VCR days), could literally recite pages of the script verbatim, had every inch of his bedroom covered with *Star Wars* posters, and faithfully dressed as a Jedi knight every Halloween. Obsessed? No, he was simply enchanted. *Star Wars* resonated with something in this young man that reassured him that good could triumph over evil, that ordinary people could make a difference, and that individuals of vastly different cultures and backgrounds could work together toward a common goal.

Sports can cast the same spell of enchantment. When your children become deeply involved in their sports experiences and feel closely connected to their "sports mates," they capture the true spirit of sports.

What do we mean by having children "deeply involved" in their sports experience? We do not mean collecting every trading card known to humankind. Rather, children become deeply involved in what they do when they exercise the courage and confidence to chart their own paths, when they no longer need to look to the bench or to the stands for reassurance. They "flow" with the game because they have developed the ability to gain inner satisfaction from how well they execute their skills. They feel no distraction from images of themselves on the bench or on the victory stand. The most fulfilled athletes, first and foremost, enjoy the thrill of meeting the challenges of competition. Only then do they allow themselves to enjoy the cheers and the awards.

Your children will more likely feel closely connected to their sports community when they establish close connections with those with whom they play—both teammates and opponents. Generally, children more easily form relationships with others when they have had relationship-building experiences within their families—in other words, when family experiences have taught them how to express concern and care for others, share, forgive, work toward common goals, play fair, establish win-win situations, and give credit where credit is due.

When athletes, families, and coaches work together to establish a climate that encourages individuals to invest in both the sports activity itself and in the people who participate in it, then inspiring sports communities form, and sports become more engaging and memorable for everyone who invests themselves in taking sports to a higher level. The rewards lie in the activity of sports, not in the recognition earned.

37

DEVELOP RITUALS OF CELEBRATION

Sports provide you with opportunities to participate
in creating rituals that connect family members to
each other and to the larger community.

Pulitzer Prize-winning author Doris Kearns Goodwin
once wrote of how her father introduced her to a lifetime love
of baseball. She was six years old, Goodwin recounted, when
her father gave her a little red score book and explained to her
the intricate symbols, numbers, and letters that were the score
keeper's art. All through the summer, Goodwin would listen to
games on the radio, carefully making notations in her book.
After dinner, she would sit with her father and recount the day's
plays.

By the time Goodwin married and had children of her own,
her father had passed away, but she found herself re-enacting

the familiar rituals of baseball with her sons. She took her oldest son to spring training. She taught the youngest ones how to keep score. "When I open my eyes and see my sons in the place where my father once sat, I feel an invisible bond among our three generations," Goodwin explained, "...an anchor of loyalty and love linking my sons to the grandfather whose face they have never seen but whose person they have come to know through this most timeless of sports."

We all have an intrinsic need to feel connected to one another. That is why we have created and perpetuated rituals. The rituals carried on from one generation to the next help people feel connected to the past, the present, and the future. As other social institutions—churches, schools, and so on—continue to lose their ability to fulfill this essential need, youth sports have assumed more and more responsibility for filling the gap.

The rituals associated with sports provide opportunities for athletes, coaches, parents, and spectators to satisfy their need to feel closely connected to their friends, families, and communities. The lore of sports allows young athletes to place themselves in the cycle of history alongside those sports heroes who have gone before them.

Children begin to learn rituals at a very young age. We both have three-year-old grandsons who have already learned to imitate the rituals they witness at sporting events. They give "high fives"; they stand quietly for the national anthem; they imitate the cheers, the celebrations after great plays, and the mascot's routines. These rituals connect participants, not only to the sport itself, but also to one other and to the wider community. Through these rituals they create shared meanings and experiences that allow them to bond with fellow sports families.

You will find that among the sports rituals your family shares, some just kind of "evolve," while others—like Doris Goodwin's little red score book—require more planning and effort. Either way, do not overlook the importance of establishing family sports rituals. Both you and your children benefit when you participate in the creation and perpetuation of meaningful rituals in your youth sports communities.

Bridge the Distance

DEVELOPING A COMPASSIONATE SPORTS FAMILY

*Sports provide you and your family with opportunities
to help bridge social barriers between individuals of
different gender, ability, age, geographic location, racial
and economic background, and sexual orientation.*

Sports, like no other social institution today, have the capacity for bridging the distance between a diversity of people: men and women, young and old, gay and straight, black and white, rich and poor, and the many others who make up the fabric of American life. Since most children find so few chances to connect with those different from themselves, take full advantage of the opportunities sports provide for you and your children to broaden your range of cultural experiences. Through your initiatives, you can help your children develop responsible attitudes toward the opposite sex, address gender equity issues in school sports, bridge the generation gap, understand prejudices against homosexuals in the sports world, and cope with racism in sports. The benefits of working with your children to bridge the distance go beyond helping them learn to be more inclusive. Youth sports provide you and your family opportunities to mend, on a small scale, some of the painful fractures that exist in our culturally diverse world. This journey outside your normal boundaries will enrich your family's life beyond measure.

Principles For Bridging the Distance

HELP YOUR CHILDREN DEVELOP RESPECT FOR THE OPPOSITE SEX

Help your children understand how commonly
held gender-role stereotypes can impact
their relationships with the opposite sex.

Sports, masculinity, and sexual conquest have long
been closely linked in our society. This linkage seems to be
related to the "myth of male superiority" that has long been a
central feature of the male sports culture.

As long as the male sports community continues to per-
petuate this myth, we should not be surprised to find some
male athletes who leap to the conclusion that, not only are

they superior to women, but they also have the right to exploit them to satisfy their sexual appetites.

How pervasive this attitude becomes depends largely upon young athletes' role models. Unfortunately, the sexual conquests, appetites, and exploits of prominent male athletes have been highly exploited by the media. High-profile professional and collegiate athletes have been indicted and prosecuted for rape and other kinds of sexual assault. Even high school athletes have used their "star" status to take sexual advantage of young girls. These incidents in sports lead us to believe that there is reason for you, as a sports parent, to be on guard for signs that your son may be falling under the influence of these toxic traditions.

Positive sports parenting requires that you make a concerted effort to monitor and influence your children's sports culture so that your children do not become carriers of attitudes and beliefs that justify sexual exploitation. You need to battle against the "boys will be boys" attitude that too often prevails in sports and society.

Parents of female athletes are not without responsibility for addressing the issue of developing wholesome attitudes toward members of the opposite sex. Like other young women, female athletes can also be tempted to buy into the myth of male superiority. In spite of the fact that many athletic girls develop a level of personal confidence that allows them to reject this dysfunctional myth, they are still at risk of being sexually exploited by their male counterparts. The persistent stereotype of the female athlete as manly and lesbian compels some girls to feel they have to demonstrate their attractiveness and prove their femininity by being sexually available. The combination of the male athlete's sense of privilege and the female athlete's need to affirm her femininity can be a recipe for careless sexual adventurism.

As a positive sports parent, you have the responsibility for helping both your sons and daughters battle against cultural standards that result in one gender taking advantage of the other. Equip your children with the ability to rise above gender stereotypes that can limit their growth and development. Through modeling respect for members of the opposite sex, you can do much to help your children fight gender-role expectations that are perpetuated throughout the sports community.

39

ADDRESS GENDER EQUITY ISSUES IN SCHOOL SPORTS

Guard against gender inequities in school sports policies and practices.

Thirty years ago, it was standard to see the bulk of a school's athletic funding go toward the support of boys' sports. However, girls' greater involvement in athletics and willingness to challenge their treatment eventually led to the creation of Title IX (a federal act saying schools could not receive federal monies unless they provided equal opportunities for male and female athletes).

Today, Title IX has inspired important steps toward creating gender equity in school sports programs. However, in spite of many gains, significant discrepancies remain. These disparities persist, in part, because the parents of young female athletes allow them to. Positive sports parents need to be involved enough in school sports programs to recognize and take action when the girls' sports program is slighted by school policies and practices.

What actions should you take when you suspect inequities between male and female athletic programs?

- Thoroughly research the situation before claiming an injustice;

- Give school administrators the opportunity to explain the reasoning behind policies or practices that appear discriminatory;

- Consult with the girls' coach(es) to gain consent and/or support before taking corrective action;

- Inform and organize other parents to work toward solving the problem.

If you cannot influence changes in policy, consider legal counsel to determine the merits of your case and what other avenues of redress might be available. (There are sources of legal assistance for pursuing and filing Title IX grievances and/ or suits.) Fortunately, the pursuit of legal avenues is seldom necessary, since most school administrators and boards of education are attuned to the requirements of our times and are supportive of the goal of achieving gender equity in girls' sports.

HELP YOUR CHILDREN BRIDGE
THE GENERATION GAP

Assume responsibility for helping your children gain a
better understanding of previous generations.

Hanging on the library wall of one of the writers of this
book is an 1888 photo of the Marysville Base Ball Club, featur-
ing the author's grandfather, resplendent in 19th century baseball gear. This picture is not only a cherished family heirloom,
but also serves to provide the author with a sense of connec-
tion not only to his own sports heritage, but also to the long
history of sports in America. Such memorabilia not only reminds
us of sports' constant state of evolution, but also provides us
with a valuable sense of continuity. In the midst of rapid change,
the core structure of sport remains the same.

Each generation experiences sports differently. The grand-parents of many of today's athletes first experienced sports in the days prior to television. They learned to imagine what was happening on the playing field by listening to radio accounts of games. More than likely, they lacked organized sports programs and instead learned their sports skills in the streets or on vacant lots. And for the women of that era, sports opportunities were few and fleeting.

Parents of today's young athletes have always known TV sports, but many (especially moms) lacked access to the rich range of organized sports experiences currently available to young people. Moms who did participate in sports may be able to share with their children the ups and downs of being the first girl to play on a boy's Little League team or to join the wrestling squad.

Despite differing experiences, sports are among the few interests upon which generations can find a common ground. Sharing sports memories and photographs and describing the achievements of sports legends can serve as an effective way for older and younger generations to connect with each other. Grandpa talking of the first time he saw Mickey Mantle play, and grandson sharing his thrill at seeing Mark McGwire break the home-run record build bridges that span the decades and link the past with the future.

Children need to understand and appreciate the experi-ences of the people who have gone before them; after all, those experiences shaped the world in which they now live. Take the time to make it possible for your children to be enriched by connecting with and gaining from the experiences of those who have lived and competed in a bygone era.

HELP YOUR CHILDREN DEVELOP A BETTER UNDERSTANDING OF HOMOSEXUALITY IN THE SPORTS WORLD

Parents need to deal openly with the issue of homosexuality, teach their children how to accept differences, and treat all sports participants with dignity and respect, regardless of their sexual orientation.

Until recently, the issue of homosexuality in sports was not something that was openly discussed. We understand that this issue is very complicated and sensitive for many families. Because this issue is so closely related to each family's fundamental values and beliefs, it is your responsibility as a positive sports parent to bring the issue into the open and help your children come to grips with it as it relates to their lives in sports. Neither you nor your children will gain anything from ignoring the homosexual presence in sports and the challenges it presents.

For decades, sports leaders have made a concerted effort to: 1) deny that homosexuality exists in men's sports; and 2) battle the stereotype of female athletes as being "manly" and/ or lesbian. At this point in the history of American sports, homosexuality is an issue that continues to generate strong feelings and great confusion for many female athletes and their parents, as well as for gay male athletes.

How can you, as a positive sports parent, help your children deal with this issue? How should you guide your sons and daughters through a world where homosexuality remains a potential stigma for women athletes who choose sports careers, and a continuing source of anguish for all young gay and lesbian athletes?

First, you must invest in coming to a better understanding of the issue yourself. You need to understand that whether your daughter is straight or gay, there is a high probability that she will be in some way affected by prejudices against female athletes. You also need to understand that, while most male athletes are not affected by the issue of homosexuality in sports, gay male athletes are often the object of discrimination, harassment, and violence.

Second, you need to challenge the gay stereotype whenever it appears in your children's sports programs. Stereotypes are damaging to your children's ability to effectively relate to others who experience the world differently.

Third, you must guard against efforts by anyone who is

promoting practices that seek to advance "hyper-masculine" images of male athletes or "hyper-feminine" images of female athletes. For example, if your son's coach warns him not to cry because that is what "sissies" do, or your daughter's teammates avoid weight training because it would make them "look too much like guys," then step in and tell your children that neither crying nor lifting weights make them any more or less masculine or feminine.

Regardless of your feelings about homosexuality, your commitment to using sports as a place to learn life's lessons requires that you use this issue to communicate the importance of treating everyone with dignity and respect. Dealing openly with the issue of homosexuality in sports provides excellent opportunities to accept differences, advance your family's values, and broaden your children's understanding of the realities of today's world.

42

HELP YOUR CHILDREN COPE WITH RACISM IN YOUTH SPORTS

You are responsible for teaching your children to accept and appreciate people different from themselves: their teammates, opponents, coaches, and other team parents, regardless of their racial or ethnic background.

In 1998, the University of Utah's Final Four victory over North Carolina was tarnished when one of the Tar Heels claimed that a Utah player uttered racial slurs toward him during the game. The North Carolina player later recanted his statement and apologized to his opponent. However, the incident served to point out an issue that many sports fans would prefer to ignore: Racism is alive and well in America's sports programs.

When we watch professional sports on television, we might

easily conclude that racism no longer exists in sports. While the hurdles have truly been lowered for minorities to enter the world of sports, few minorities find leadership positions—head coaches, general managers, and so on. In addition, youth sports in America are, by and large, still segregated, which may well stem from the fact that youth sports are typically neighborhood-based. If a neighborhood is predominantly white, black, Hispanic, or whatever, its youth sports team will reflect the same make-up. In some cases, because of the regional groupings of teams (ostensibly to reduce travel time for competition), entire leagues are segregated. This reality presents a significant challenge to parents who want to use sports as a way of introducing their children to the cultural and racial diversity that makes our country strong.

Sports can provide families with a rich opportunity to break down traditional racial stereotypes, allowing athletes of different races to become better acquainted. Sports can become a basis upon which people of different racial, economic, and cultural backgrounds find a common ground.

However, these changes happen only with parental effort and influence. If you want to use sports as a means of fighting racism, participate in shaping policies that define the geographic boundaries of youth sports leagues. Find ways of ensuring that children who want to participate in youth sports can do so, even if their families are unable to afford it. (Because of high school federation and NCAA rules regarding the prohibition of economic benefits to high school athletes, youth sports clubs sometimes have to find imaginative ways of adhering to the spirit of the rules, while at the same time providing opportunities for children for whom participation is not economically feasible.)

Most of all, set the example for your children that you will not tolerate racism in your home or on the athletic field. Sports should provide people an escape from these cruelties and injustices of the world. They should represent opportunities for athletes to play with and against each other without considering the color of each other's skin. It is up to you to make it so.

PART 6

Take the Lead

ASSUMING LEADERSHIP IN YOUR CHILDREN'S SPORTS COMMUNITY

When you serve as a parent leader for your children's teams, you find many opportunities to create positive experiences for the entire sports community.

Youth sports in America are heavily dependent upon volunteer parent labor. It is therefore essential that you lend your time and talents in serving as fund raisers, coaches, referees, chaperones, and program administrators. Rather than seeing these roles as a burden, view them as opportunities to imprint your children's youth sports programs with the ideas and values of a positive sports parent. Assuming a leadership role gives you the opportunity to support positive coaching

behavior, help young athletes make appropriate choices, encourage other parents to participate fully in their children's sports
experiences, and strengthen and unify your sports community.
It also allows you to serve as an example to your own family
and others of the joy that comes through working to make a
positive difference in others' lives.

Principles for Taking The Lead

43

DEVELOP A WORKING RELATIONSHIP WITH THE COACH

Understand and respect the responsibilities of the coach, and work to establish a cooperative and supportive relationship between the coach and team parents.

Sometimes we as parents need to be reminded that coaches are people, too, that they have families and responsibilities that extend beyond the sports field. We may also forget that a coach's time with his or her athletes is extremely limited—at best, coaches spend a couple of hours a day, five days per week during the season. Still, we often expect the coach to be closely attuned to each and every athlete's needs (especially our own son or daughter). This attitude puts a tremendous burden on the coach and may lead to a tense relationship between coaches and parents.

In successful youth programs (the ones that we have observed, anyway), a parent or parents take the lead in acting as a liaison between the coach and other parents in the program. These parent leaders serve as a conduit to help parents better understand the philosophy of the coach and the limitations of the program in accommodating unique family needs. They also serve as a buffer between the parents and the coach, to help ensure that what little time the coach does have is spent primarily on coaching duties.

Effective parent leaders are those who

- Take the time to understand the coach's philosophy, style, and personality;

- Understand how the coach defines his or her role as well as the roles of the parent leader(s), and the other parents;

- Understand what the other parents expect from the coach and the parent leader(s);

- Can help the coach and parents work through differences in perspective (such as when the coach's primary interest is in producing a winning team and the parents are more concerned with advancing their children's appreciation of the game);

- Assume responsibility for ensuring that differences of opinions between coach and parents are resolved in a civil and considerate manner;

- Remind parents that the coach's role is to coach and the parents' role is to offer counsel and provide administrative assistance (when asked) to help the program run smoothly; and

- Insist on a spirit of cooperation and good will between coach and parents.

It is impossible to achieve and/or maintain a positive sports environment when parents and coaches are at odds with one another. By making the effort to establish a positive working relationship with your child's coach, you can make the sports experience more enjoyable for your family and for others in your sports program.

SUPPORT POSITIVE COACHING BEHAVIOR

Work with the coaches to ensure the use
of positive teaching methods.

In a perfect world, coaches would be enlightened, caring individuals who are inclined to use positive coaching methods to teach and inspire each young athlete to do his or her best, both as athletes and as human beings.

Fortunately for our children, most coaches do fit this model. However, as we noted earlier, some coaches have been known to physically, psychologically, or sexually abuse the athletes in their care.

Identifying such abuse can be difficult. Nevertheless, you have the responsibility to remain vigilant to evidence that children—whether they are your own or someone else's—are being mistreated by their coach.

As a parent leader, you have the responsibility of working with the other parents to establish reasonable standards for assessing coaching effectiveness. You have the responsibility for taking initiatives on behalf of the parent community to collaborate with the coach to ensure that nothing is keeping sports from being an uplifting and renewing experience for both athletes and their families. If a parent complains to a parent leader about a coach, then it is the parent leader's responsibility to gather information from the complaining parent and submit it to the coach, with the request that the coach address the issue directly with the parent whose child has initiated the complaint.

In addition, a parent leader who witnesses an opposing coach abusing an athlete should file a complaint directly with the coach, as well as report the incident to the coach's superior or the event manager.

When engaged in an evaluation of coaches, whether it be their own coach or others, parent leaders must also take care to protect the rights of coaches. Sometimes what is thought to be abuse (such as when a child complains that "coach made us practice all afternoon in the hot sun with no water") is merely a misunderstanding or oversight on the part of either the coach or the athlete.

One of the most helpful things parent leaders can do is to help other parents not only recognize signs of excessive training or abuse, but also to recognize and reward positive coaching behavior. Signs of positive coaching include

- The coach knows each athlete by name within the first few practices;
- The coach speaks respectfully to all athletes;
- The coach rotates players so everyone gets several chances to play;
- The coach recognizes the abilities and limitations of all athletes;
- The coach uses positive, not negative, reinforcement to encourage athletes; and
- The athletes are having fun!

The bottom line is that parent leaders and other concerned individuals must take every effort to curb the cancer of coaching excesses and abuses and to preserve youth sports as a place where children and families can have fun and enjoy the thrill of collective accomplishment.

45

HELP INTEGRATE THE ISOLATED ATHLETE INTO THE LIFE OF THE TEAM

Be vigilant to the social dynamics of the team, and make sure everyone feels included.

Our country witnessed a chilling example of how deeply children can feel the effects of being social outcasts when two disaffected young men walked into their high school in Littleton, Colorado, and gunned down twelve of their schoolmates and one teacher.

On a typical sports team, it is not unusual for one or more athletes to be excluded from the central social group. The consequences of players being isolated by the "inner circle" can be damaging to both the isolated athlete and to the team's chemistry. When you, as a parent leader, sense that an athlete is being isolated by other members of the team, take the responsibility to report the situation to the coach, and work with him or her to better integrate the child into the mainstream of the team.

We all know that children (especially teenagers) can be exceptionally cruel when one of their peers does not conform to their expected pattern of behavior. The athlete may be socially awkward, culturally different, may speak differently, have a distinctive look, wear different clothes, or behave in any number of ways that do not conform to what other team members expect and are comfortable with. Or it might be that the isolated child is someone viewed as receiving "special treatment" from the coach.

In dealing with the problem of an athlete ostracized by teammates, you, as a parent leader, need to ask, "Who has the problem?" Does the isolated child have the problem, or does the problem reside with the rest of the team—that is, with their inability to tolerate non-conformity? In most cases, the problem lies with both. The isolated child realizes that he or she does not have the support of the rest of the team, and that impacts his or her ability to contribute to achieving team goals. And the rest of the team suffers, not only because their individual capacity to develop compassion and understanding is impeded, but also because they cannot come together as a team, which in turn diminishes their prospects for team success.

You can accomplish a great deal when you and the coach collaborate in trying to integrate the ostracized child into the social fabric of the team. For example, the coach can construct on-court drills that put the isolated child in a position to earn the respect of teammates. Either you or the coach can choose to talk privately with one of the team leaders to solicit help in making the isolated child feel more included. You can work to make sure the athletes include everyone in the team's informal activities. You can take a special interest in the isolated child and his or her family. By demonstrating a willingness to include the isolated child in your family's life, you communicate a powerful message to the rest of the team.

46

HELP TEAM MEMBERS COMMUNICATE WITH THEIR COACH

Develop strategies for facilitating
communication between athletes and coaches.

As children work to establish their own identities independent of the adults in their lives, communication problems
often develop. For the most part, we, the parents, bear the
brunt of our children's resistance to our efforts to influence them,
but coaches are not immune to their resistance, either. That is
why you may find it useful as a parent leader—who is not
regularly putting the athletes through their paces—to facilitate
communication between the athletes and the coach.

To become a conduit for communication between the
athletes and the coach, you must earn the trust of both. Demonstrate that you are caring, reliable, and can be counted on to

maintain a confidence. Both the coach and the athletes need to be assured that you will not reveal to anyone what they share with you without first securing their consent.

You can gain their confidence by listening attentively to what both the athletes and the coach are saying, without passing judgment on either. As soon as you begin passing judgment ("Hey, guys, don't you think you're being a little hard on the coach? I'm sure that's not what he really said, was it?"), you align yourself with the coach, and no longer can be counted upon to be an impartial observer.

As you strive to be impartial, be aware of how your actions look to the coach and to the athletes. For example, it is natural during "down" time on away trips for adults to congregate. When the coach spends most of his or her down time with you, athletes may assume that the adults are "ganging up" on them. On the other hand, if you spend all your time with the athletes, then the coach may feel that you are attempting to undercut his or her authority and take control of the team. At the same time, you do need to become well enough acquainted with the athletes that they feel they can be candid about any communication problems that might have arisen between them and the coach. You also need to know the coach well enough to understand his or her coaching style and philosophy.

One of the simplest ways for you to develop effective communication between athletes and coaches is to urge the coach to hold a team meeting to discuss issues in dispute. At these meetings, you can act as a facilitator to ensure that

- The athletes feel free to bring up concerns without fear of reprisal on the coach's part;
- The coach demonstrates an open and non-defensive attitude;
- No one scolds and/or preaches; and
- The meeting avoids turning into a group therapy session (which most coaches and parents are unequipped to administer).

47

HELP TEAM MEMBERS RESPECT PROPERTY RIGHTS

Ensure that athletes refrain from careless and destructive acts at training and competition sites.

For many years, a staunch rivalry has existed between Brigham Young University and the University of Utah. Since both schools mark their location with a huge block letter (a "Y" for BYU and a "U" for Utah) stenciled on the mountain behind them, it has been traditional for students, right before a big game between the two, to sneak up the mountain and paint the other school's letter with the opposing school colors.

However, this lighthearted fun was carried too far one year when the statue of Brigham Young that stands in the middle of BYU's campus was discovered drenched in "Utah red" paint.

Young people easily get carried away and engage in destructive acts. Athletes certainly have no immunity to this behavior, especially when they get caught up in the thrill of winning or the disappointment of losing. They sometimes deface property, set off fire alarms, toss water bombs or fire-crackers on passers by, steal corporate banners from compe-tition sites, write graffiti on restroom walls, and break items by misusing them. Any parent who has ever accompanied a group of young people on a road trip has had the chance to witness this type of immature behavior in one form or another.

One of the reasons that this kind of behavior endures is that each generation of youth hears adults recounting, with relish, tales of the legendary "high jinx" that occurred during their youth. These tales can often be interpreted as approval to steal a mascot, scribble obscenities on opponent's signs, or throw paint on a statue.

The challenge for you as a leader in youth sports is to pre-vent these actions before they happen. First, make sure that the team has specific guidelines that govern their "off the field behavior" on road trips. While it might be easier for you or the coach to prepare this "Code of Conduct," it will be more effective if you involve the athletes. You may want to identify some of the issues that need to be addressed, but the athletes themselves should identify the ways they choose to be guided by the code. The code should clearly define behaviors that will be encouraged as well as behaviors that will be discouraged.

Besides defining what constitutes appropriate and inappro-priate behavior, also establish an enforcement procedure. For example, will the responsibility for enforcing the code of conduct reside with the coach and parent leader(s), or with the team? Finally, if a violation does occur, you have responsibility, in collaboration with the coach, to insist that the team follow through with the sanctions outlined in the code of conduct.

When you involve athletes in setting and enforcing standards of conduct, you take an important step toward preventing violations of good judgment. In other words, you have not simply drafted a guiding document—you have allowed the team to agree on what they expect of one another. These peer expectations can be far more influential than any parental lecture.

48

HELP PARENTS APPRECIATE THE BENEFITS OF POSITIVE SPORTS PARENTING

Assume responsibility for encouraging
parent behavior that contributes to an
atmosphere of mutual respect and conviviality.

Attending your child's sporting event should be a pleasure, not an ordeal. However, there are times when the behavior of other parents leaves you cringing with embarrassment,
and wondering, "What should I do about this ugly situation?"

One of the most effective ways to prevent parents from
spoiling the experiences for both the athletes and the other
parents is for you as a parent leader to take steps toward building a sense of community among families in the youth sports
program. The best time to begin is before the first team outing
of the season—that way, each parent can have a clear idea of

what is expected of him or her in terms of positive, supportive behavior.

Urge all team parents to attend pre-season meetings. At these meetings, take responsibility to make sure that, in addition to discussing such topics as fund raising and team rules, additional items appear on the agenda. First of all it, is important to address the issue of how best to demonstrate support for the team. It is essential that you discuss how you as a parent community can create a positive parental presence for the program. In these discussions consider how the athletes view parents' sideline behavior. As a result of these discussions parents should come to understand that only positive messages will motivate the athletes. When they have arrived at guidelines for providing positive support for their children, seek consensus among the parents as to what types of comments from the sidelines are most likely to get the desired results on the playing field and which types are likely to be distracting to the athletes.

As a group, parents can decide how they want to handle offensive behavior, should it occur. Some leagues distribute "guidelines for spectator conduct." Your group may want to draw up your own code of conduct.

We have found that parents tend to adhere more closely to a set of standards that they helped create, rather than being dictated to from "on high." An approach that emphasizes creating a positive parental presence from the beginning is more effective than having to sanction a zealous parent who has gotten carried away in the heat of the moment. These interruptions can unintentionally damage the team's effectiveness and dampen the other parents' enthusiasm for being involved with the program.

Parents should be able to leave a competition not only feeling uplifted by the experience of witnessing their children's accomplishments, but also inspired by being a participant in a community of parents who shares common interests and values. When parents work together to make sports a positive experience, sports truly become a celebration and an affirmation for everyone involved.

49

BE SENSITIVE TO THE INDIVIDUAL NEEDS OF EACH FAMILY

Find ways to accommodate and include working mothers
and single-parent families in your team community.

It has been a long time since traditional, two-parents-with-a-stay-at-home-mom families were the norm in America. Today, we have more than 11.4 million single parents in our country, while nearly 80 percent of mothers of school-age children work outside the home.

Participation in youth sports presents special challenges for these families whose time and resources may be severely limited. It also presents challenges for coaches and parent leaders, who may begin to feel resentful of families whom they feel contribute less than their "fair share" to the youth sports program.

It is not uncommon for very busy parents to use the youth sports program as a baby-sitting service. That is not to say that families with stay-at-home moms do not take advantage of youth sports leaders in the same way; some do. Nor is it to say that stay-at-home moms are not gainfully occupied with other service and/or work-related activities. We are simply pointing out that parent leaders and coaches need to make an effort to work around the limitations that each family brings to the team.

Rather than feeling resentment in these situations, try to view this social and economic reality as an opportunity for the youth sports community to reach out and embrace those families whose circumstances might not allow them to invest a lot of time in neighborhood-based sports.

We have found that working mothers and single-parent families who are warmly invited into the youth sports community benefit greatly from their investment in their children's sports lives. This is especially true when they are included in ways that fit within the everyday demands of their lives. For example, it may not be possible for single parents or working moms to participate in team activities during the week, but you can ask them to join the other parents on weekend team outings.

Take care, however, that your gestures of accommodation are not seen as "charity." Rather, they should represent a natural outgrowth of your efforts to include all families, regardless of their employment, marital or economic status, in the sports community.

One way to make sure parents have the opportunity to contribute to their children's sports experiences is to pass out a survey at the beginning of the season, listing different activities (e.g., bringing treats to games, calling parents, making banners, driving kids to or from practice) and to ask parents to choose which ones they can fit into their schedules.

It is not growth-enhancing if only intact or affluent families are active in the sports community, or if the team leadership includes only the stay-at-home moms, or if the end-of-season party resembles a "couples-only" affair. Just as we want our children to learn to get along with a variety of teammates, we parents need to set the example by reaching out to and including everyone in the sports community.

50

ENCOURAGE PARENTAL INVOLVEMENT IN YOUTH SPORTS PROGRAMS

Invite team parents to play an active role in supporting their children's sports programs.

If the number one complaint of coaches and sports administrators is how hard it is to work with parents (certain ones, anyway!), then the number two complaint is how hard it is to work without parents. In other words, it is difficult to run an effective youth sports program without parental involvement.

When properly orchestrated, parent participation can greatly enhance a program and result in significant dividends for the parents who make the effort to contribute. That is why it is essential that some level of parental involvement, such as attendance at a mandatory orientation session, be required in order to participate in a youth sports program. It is in these orientation sessions that coaches and administrators clearly specify what they expect of the athletes and you, their families.

If no such orientation is available, we recommend that you take the initiative and volunteer to help organize one. Doing so will not only show the coach that you are committed to making the youth sports experience the best that it can be, but will also serve as an example to other parents who may be less inclined to get involved in their children's sports programs.

The parents with the greatest chance of charting a new direction for parental participation are those who demonstrate their willingness to work for the program, who have records of effective leadership, and whose children are the mainstays on the team.

Of course, while most coaches would give their right arm to have a group of committed, caring parents working with them, some are more ambivalent. Coaches who have had negative experiences with parents in the past sometimes consciously or unconsciously discourage parent participation. That is why you need to make sure that your responsibilities do not include those that belong to the coach, such as selecting the team, designing the practice plans, administering the games, making substitutions, and sanctioning players who fail to abide by team rules.

However, the most resistance to parental involvement will probably come from other parents. You will hear a variety of reasons, number one most likely being "I just don't have the time!" Be patient, and (as mentioned in the previous principle) try to provide a variety of ways that parents can get involved according to their means. Above all, avoid communicating the attitude that participating in the youth sports program is just another "chore." When you talk about how much fun you have talking to the kids as you drive them to and from practice, or how enthusiastically the community supported the last team fund raiser, then you send the message that participating in the youth sports program can have pay offs for the whole family, not just the athlete involved.

51

HELP PARENTS BECOME STUDENTS OF THEIR CHILDREN'S SPORTS

Take initiatives to help all team parents achieve a better understanding of the games their children play.

Parents who are not properly informed about the rules, strategies, and training methods involved in their child's sports are the ones who make life difficult for the coach, other parents, and—tragically—their own child.

To avoid the problems caused by this particular group of parents, smart coaches and program administrators make sure that part of the pre-season orientation includes at least one session where parents are introduced to

- The coach's philosophy and training methods;
- Basic rules and strategies of the game; and

- Drills that the athletes will be expected to master (parents should be required to "walk through" these drills so they have a better understanding of what is involved).

Very few youth sports programs actually require parents to achieve this kind of minimal mastery of the game. However, it is a simple fact that the more knowledgeable a person is about a subject, the more she or he will enjoy that subject. Parents who have the opportunity to learn more about the games their children play will find more enjoyment.

If your child's sports program does not provide this or a similar type of parent orientation, then you should take the initiative in making sure it does. One way to do so is to approach the coach or program administrator and say, "My sports knowledge isn't as sharp as it could be, and I'm sure other parents feel the same way. Could you help us be better informed so that we don't end up teaching our children the wrong things?"

Your next step should be to encourage other parents to participate in the orientation session(s). Consider a friendly phone call or something as light-hearted as a flyer advertising, "Everything You Always Wanted to Know About Your Child's Sport but Were Afraid to Ask!"

Also consider working with administrators to carefully plan the orientation session(s). The goal is to make sure parents are informed, not embarrassed. The session should be a fun time for both parents and the coach, and not an occasion for anyone to "strut their stuff."

When parents are given the opportunity to increase their knowledge in a joyful and mutually supportive atmosphere, they will bond more closely with other team parents and establish a foundation for creating a more supportive and positive sports environment for everyone.

52

HELP FAMILIES UNDERSTAND THE VALUE OF TEAM LOYALTY

By building a solid sense of community, you can help team parents avoid the negative consequences that occur when their children jump from one team to another.

What would happen if professional team athletes—like football, basketball, or baseball players—could play for any team they chose, at any time? Players would immediately flock to those teams that could offer them the best package. Big city teams in desirable locations (like Los Angeles or New York) would flourish, while teams in places like Minnesota or Utah would probably have to make do with players not good enough to be signed anywhere else. Among others, these reasons compel professional sports leagues to use contracts, the draft, and salary caps, hopefully making the playing field more-or-less equal.

Youth sports are different. While most leagues and federations have restrictions on athletes transferring from one program to another, you (for the most part) do have the freedom to choose where you want your child to participate. Parents of highly talented young athletes occasionally move to a different school district or transport their children to a club in a different community, simply to allow their children to participate in what the parents feel is a "better" program.

Unfortunately, families who make these changes seldom consider the consequences of their decisions on the remaining athletes and their families. All youth sports families will benefit from understanding that such decisions are not made in a vacuum. For example, when a star player leaves a team, the remaining players have often lost their leader. This loss diminishes their chances for success as a team and reduces their prospects for winning college scholarships. In addition, the move may disrupt the chemistry of the athlete's "new" team, and the athlete may find that he or she now occupies a reduced role on the new team.

As a parent leader, you can guard against team-jumping. Your best safeguard is building a solid sense of community among the team families. Much less team jumping occurs when all families feel committed to one another. Team families hesitate to leave a social environment they feel they have helped shape.

We also recommend holding parent meetings (with the coach's approval) at various points during the season, where you and other parents may discuss these and other issues with the potential to impact the team. Remember that lectures about loyalty frequently fail to build mutual commitment. Instead, team loyalty grows from discussions about shared expectations and how to create the ideal team climate.

Ultimately, urge parents thinking of moving their child from one team to another to consider more than their child's opportunities to be a starter or to win a championship on a new team. Invite them to consider what values team-jumping teaches a young athlete and what message it sends to the families on the team left behind. Unfortunately, once thoughts of leaving the team become serious, few efforts will likely make a difference. Avoid this situation by addressing team-jumping *before* an opportunity arises.

Establish Your Own Positive Sports Parenting Program!

You are committed to taking sports to a higher level, but how can your school or club join you in creating a youth sports climate that brings the best out of everyone—athletes, coaches, and parents? The Positive Sports Parenting Program provides hands-on advice for guiding children to experiencing sports in ways that not only build their bodies, but enrich their lives, too!

Starting a Positive Sports Parenting Program in your community is easy!

Step 1: Tell your local youth sports leader (perhaps a school administrator or club director) about Positive Sports Parenting and ask that leader to contact the Positive Sports Parenting national office at (281) 565-2234.

Step 2: We will help your local youth sports leader identify two to four parents who will receive specialized training from the Positive Sports Parenting staff. This training prepares parents to become Positive Sports Parenting Program Leaders.

Step 3: The Positive Sports Parenting Program Leaders will recruit and train additional parents to become High-Five Team Facilitators.

Step 4: High-Five Team Facilitators will use this book, <u>From the Bleachers with Love,</u> along with a companion workbook, to hold sports parenting workshops with small groups of parents within the school, club, or team.

Take the first step toward more Positive Sports Parenting for your children!

CONTACT:
Positive Sports Parenting • P.O. Box 1429 • Sugar Land, TX 77478
Phone (281) 565-2234 •Fax (281) 565-2224